INSIDE JAZZ

(ORIGINALLY PUBLISHED AS
INSIDE BE-BOP)

by

LEONARD FEATHER

With a New Introduction

A DA CAPO PAPERBACK

Library of Congress Cataloging in Publication Data

Feather, Leonard G
   Inside jazz.

   (The Roots of jazz)
   Reprint of the 1949 ed. published by J. J. Robbins,
New York, under title: Inside be-bop.
   Discography: p.
   1. Jazz music. 2. Jazz musicians. 3. Jazz music—
Discography. I. Title. II. Title: Inside be-bop.
ML3561.J3F4 1977   785.4'2   77-23411
ISBN 0-306-80076-4 (pbk.)

ISBN: 0-306-80076-4

First Da Capo Paperback Edition — October, 1977
Second Da Capo Paperback — April, 1980

This Da Capo Press paperback edition of *Inside Jazz* is an unabridged republication,
with the exception of a new introduction by the author, of the first edition published
in New York in 1949 under the title *Inside Be-bop* and later reprinted under the title
Inside Jazz. It is reprinted by arrangement with Consolidated Music Publishers.

Published by Da Capo Press, Inc.
A Subsidiary of Plenum Publishing Corporation
227 West 17th Street, New York, N.Y. 10011

Introduction to the New Edition

Inside Be-bop was first published under that title by J.J. Robbins & Sons, Inc. in 1949. A couple of years later the publisher, scared by the supposedly pejorative significance of this much maligned term, changed its name to *Inside Jazz*. The book itself remained identical; only the cursed implications of that hated word were removed. It continued to sell in small quantities but went underground in the late 1950s and by the turn of the decade had disappeared entirely—unlike the music itself, which has remained as alive as it was the day the book came out.

Inside Jazz has become probably the most quoted book in jazz history. Perhaps *plagiarized* would be a better word, for whole passages, particularly those in the Charlie Parker chapter, have been printed time and time again elsewhere without credit. It is a pleasure to see the original stories presented here in the form in which they first appeared.

At the time of its publication, jazz literature was in a sorry state. There had been very few books on the subject in the English language; in fact, strange as it may seem to the young student today, *Inside Be-bop* was the first book complete with technical data ever written by an author with empirical experience as a jazz musician and composer. I am not counting such early volumes as the Louis Armstrong and Benny Goodman biographies, both written with co-authors, both published in the late 1930s and involving no musicological or technical investigation.

My book owed its existence to Jack Robbins. A veteran music man who had sold his great publishing empire and started a smaller company, he was the only man in this generally myopic field to show some sympathy for and understanding of the new jazz, and to publish music by some of its composers. For the same reason he agreed that a book devoted to the movement, and subdivided in the manner seen here (*When,* a historical recounting of the bop era; *How,* a technical analysis of the music itself; and *Who,* an alphabetical/biographical rundown of its principal exponents), would find a viable market.

In order to understand the difficulties entailed in writing and publishing this book, it is necessary for the reader to be aware of the incredible climate of hostility that existed when bop began to take on significance and to be played extensively by the young musicians of the day. The half dozen quotes used as a sort of prelude to the book are fairly representative. It did not matter that Sigmund Spaeth, a rather typically square classical musicologist and educator of his day, took such a dim view of bop; after all, he was the composer of such masterpieces as "Honolulu Lulu," "Jabberwocky" and "The Old Barbershop," so it was difficult to take any of his views seriously. Nor did anybody care what Jimmy Cannon or the *Moscow Literary Gazette* had to say. But when such respectable critics as John Hammond and George Frazier took an aggressive anti-bop stance, they had to be reckoned with, since their opinions were generally more respected. As for Tommy Dorsey, it was he, not bebop, who set music back. In the late 1940s he was the host of a syndicated disc jockey show; I worked for him for a while and recall that he steadfastly refused either to have Dizzy Gillespie as a guest or to play any records of what to him was a reprehensible form of music.

Aside from the younger jazz musicians themselves, the supporters of bop were a small and lonely minority. The only publication to champion the cause actively was *Metronome,* a monthly magazine of which Barry Ulanov and I were co-editors during the middle and late 1940s. I was also able to establish a major area of exposure for progressive music and musicology through *Esquire* magazine. My collaboration with Robert Goffin, a Belgian jazz critic, and Arnold Gingrich, *Esquire's* editor at that time, led to the establishment of the first jazz critics' poll and the staging of concerts at which the winners took part in an all-star jam session. It was in *Esquire* and its annual jazz yearbooks that such musicians as Dizzy Gillespie, Charlie Parker, J.J. Johnson and Milt Jackson won their first awards. A few of the great young musicians of the day, such as Lucky Thompson, won their *only* award in the *Esquire* Poll.

The feud between the beboppers and the so-called "moldy figs" (advocates of the traditional New Orleans jazz played by veteran trumpeter Bunk Johnson, clarinetist George Lewis and others of the revivalist movement that became active around the same time as bebop) was aggravated by the fact that instead of just advocating our own cause, Barry and I also wasted time making fun of the figs, whose movement would eventually collapse of its own weight. Our satires on the old time jazz aficionados, particularly those I wrote under the name of Professor McSiegel, infuriated the traditionalists, who lambasted modern jazz in general and bop in particular.

For every attack by what the figs thought of as "the *Metronome-Esquire*-Feather-Ulanov axis," there would be an equally virulent counterattack, usually in the pages of *The Record Changer,* a magazine fanatically dedicated to the right wing (this was before Orrin Keepnews and Bill Grauer took it over and brought it into the 20th century). These conditions changed gradually, as the impact of bop became so evident that national magazines finally recognized it in print (see page 43). *Inside Be-bop* went to press at a crucial time, just before the pivotal Miles Davis "Birth of the Cool" sessions. (Gil Evans, a key figure in that movement, is the one musician conspicuous by his absence in the book.)

A few months after the publication of *Inside Be-bop,* Birdland opened. It was the end of the decade (December 1949) and the beginning of a new era for modern jazz in nightclubs. Birdland became "the jazz corner of the world." Bop groups found a haven there; later the movement known as "hard bop," best represented by Art Blakey and his Jazz Messengers, also found support at Birdland and other comparable clubs around the country.

By the early 1950s new combos had been established whose soloists were essentially grounded in bop: the George Shearing Quintet, the Oscar Peterson Trio, the Modern Jazz Quartet, and the combos of Miles Davis and Thelonious Monk. Thelonious, by the way, was given rather short shrift in the book; on the other hand, he was later overpraised by fanatical supporters. The truth about Monk lies halfway between the unjust early derogation and the subsequent cult-like hero worship.

Bunk Johnson died in 1949; the New Orleans revivalist movement also faded, though George Lewis, the other central figure idolized by the figs, lived until 1968 and found a loyal band of supporters at home and abroad. Meanwhile, even the death of Charlie Parker in 1955 did not slow the advance of bebop, for a couple of months later, Cannonball Adderley arrived in New York, was an immediate sensation, and was hailed as the logical successor to Bird.

Of the 92 musicians whose biographies form the final section of the book, four had died young before it was published (Sonny Berman, Jimmy Blanton, Charlie Christian, Freddy Webster). Since then, 24 more have died, not one of whom achieved the span of three score years and ten. At least half of these lives were shortened by one or other of the twin evils that were a part of the jazz night life, narcotics and alcohol. Fourteen others are in obscurity, or have moved to areas not associated with bop, including Stan Levy (professional photographer), George Wallington (in the refrigerator business), Oscar Moore (retired many years ago), John Simmons (sidelined by illness), and Miles Davis (sidelined by rock).

The rest of the 92 remain, in varying degrees, connected with the same music that was part of their image almost three decades ago when the compilation of the book got under way. Such men as Ray Brown, Conte Candoli, Sonny Criss, Buddy de Franco, Dizzy Gillespie, Dexter Gordon, Milt Jackson, Budd Johnson, Barney Kessel, John Lewis, Art Pepper, Max Roach, Sonny Stitt and dozens of others, though their styles may have expanded and their technique broadened, are living testimonials to the durability of a musical form that survived the outrage of its adversaries and went on to prove the permanence of its value.

Charlie Parker, in a sense, is more alive than ever. The group known as *Supersax,* launched in 1972, has dedicated itself to the preservation of Bird's original solos, taken off the recordings and harmonized for a five-piece saxophone section. One of the Supersax albums won a Grammy Award; their appearances at clubs and festivals have been warmly received by young fans, some of whom were not yet born when Charlie Parker died.

Dizzy Gillespie, the other half of the team that effectively set bebop in motion, will be in his sixties by the time this is read. A veteran of international tours for the State Department, honored by the citizens of his home town, he has become an elder statesman who, ironically, is regarded by some of today's less perceptive observers as a traditionalist himself. The year 1977 found him playing more brilliantly than ever, with a confidence and control born of decades of experience in bringing his art to perfection. The respect in which Gillespie is now held around the world is the ultimate answer to what once seemed like a reasonable question concerning the survival of bebop.

For more information concerning the period represented here, I recommend Ira Gitler's *Jazz Masters of the Forties,* published in 1966 by Macmillan. The book also includes recommended lists of long play records, although their availability keeps changing. Fortunately, double-LP sets continue to be reissued by Fantasy, Savoy, Blue Note and whatever other record companies own the rights to the early bebop classics. It all adds up to one basic conclusion: in concert halls, at clubs, on old records, wherever jazz is heard, bebop lives!

LEONARD FEATHER
Sherman Oaks, California
August 1977

"The gradual development (or decadence) of the distortion of jazz . . . to the artificial absurdities of the so-called 'Bebop' style must be fairly obvious even to the casual listener."

SIGMUND SPAETH

"Bebop sounds to me like a hardware store in an earthquake."

JIMMY CANNON

"Bebop has set music back twenty years."

TOMMY DORSEY

"Bebop bears the same relationship to music as tonsillitis."

LITERARY GAZETTE, Moscow

"To me, bop is a collection of nauseating clichés, repeated ad infinitum."

JOHN HAMMOND

"This is incredible stuff for a grown man to produce."

GEO. FRAZIER

I'd like to say welcome to Leonard Feather's book on the new jazz.

Leonard is one of the few who have been in our corner for years, trying to make people understand and appreciate the kind of music we believe in. He really knows the music and the people who play it, and I'm sure this book will help to make a lot of our fans better acquainted with bop.

Best of luck and success to "Inside Bebop."

DIZZY GILLESPIE

Foreword

IT WOULD BE HARD to overestimate the role that bebop has played in revolutioniz-
ing the jazz world during the past five years. Since 1943, when musicians and
jazz students around New York first became more than dimly aware of the impact
of the new ideas developed by Dizzy Gillespie and the other pioneers of the new
movement, we have seen the gradual emergence of a new generation of jazzmen.
To some musicians and fans, many of the old jazz records they cherished for years
have lost their attraction, because the advances made by bebop have made so
much that preceded it seem unimaginative and trite by comparison.

During these same five years, millions of words have been written about
bebop and its creators. A large proportion of verbiage has been wasted on the
eccentric personality angles—the goatees, berets and other superficial manifesta-
tions of the bop cult. Too few of the national magazines and newspapers that
could have devoted their space to the more serious aspects of the music have
seen fit to do so.

It is the object of this book to compensate for those omissions. In these pages
I hope to pierce the berets and find out what goes on in the heads beneath them;
to shave off the goatees and study the sounds emanating from the lips they adorn.

Obviously a project of this kind would have been impossible without a
multitude of reference sources. I should like to acknowledge my indebtedness to
Metronome, which has published many feature articles on bop stars by Barry
Ulanov, George Simon and myself; to Richard O. Boyer, author of the excellent
profile of Dizzy which appeared in 1947 in the *New Yorker;* and to the innumerable musicians who have taken time off between sets at the Royal Roost to dig
back into their memories for background data.

PART ONE

◄◄◄◄◄◄◄◄◄◄◄◄◄ ✳ ►►►►►►►►►►►►►►►

When

Chapter I

In the beginning, there was ragtime.

This book will not attempt to trace every step that has been taken since World War I ushered in a new era of dance music. Too many histories of jazz have hit the market in the past decade, most of them devoting a vast proportion of space to the dim and distant past, with very little consideration of the present and no eye at all for the future.

For the purposes of this volume, then, we'll assume that you know, or can easily find out elsewhere, how ragtime developed into jazz in the 1920's, and how the swing era brought jazz to the attention of the public in the 1930's. Let's assume that it will be safe to begin the story at the point where we can find direct links with the phenomenon of the 1940's known as bebop.

By the time this stage had been reached—in the late 1930's—the swing craze had passed its zenith. Benny Goodman's band, aided by the arrangements of Fletcher Henderson and others, had proved that a big, commercial white orchestra could play "uncommercial" jazz successfully. Until Benny had come along, big band jazz had been played by Negro orchestras, frequently under Jim Crow conditions, and by such stiff, regimented groups as Glen Gray's original Casa Loma band, which many musicians did not consider seriously as jazz at all.

Goodman reconciled jazz with the fact that musicians were involved with a utilitarian art. The world of popular songs, of Hit Parade and Tin Pan Alley products, provided music to which housewives could dust, errand boys could whistle, and ballroom frequenters could dance. Benny showed that this world could be made to overlap into the musician's world, where a jazzman thought of a new song mainly as a sequence of chords on which to base improvisations, and an arranger would orchestrate these songs in the same spirit.

Thus it developed that not only Benny, but Tommy Dorsey, Jimmy Dorsey, Artie Shaw, Harry James, Glenn Miller, Gene Krupa, even lesser names like Tommy Reynolds and Sonny Dunham, had bands that played many of their popular songs in a rhythmic, swinging style that was as close to jazz as the Goodman band of 1935 which had started this whole trend. These bands competed for jobs with the Sammy Kayes, Guy Lombardos and Blue Barrons who had virtually monopolized the more lucrative end of the dance band business, notably in smart hotel jobs, network radio shows and best-selling records.

Such orchestras as Chick Webb's, Fletcher Henderson's and Teddy Hill's, though they also conformed with what was rapidly becoming a swing stereotype, were prevented by racial discrimination from attaining the same heights. Nevertheless, Jim Crow was breaking down under the pressure of the musicians' own attitudes. Benny Goodman pioneered with the hiring of Teddy Wilson and Lionel Hampton; Shaw followed with Billie Holiday, Krupa with Leo Watson, and by 1939 a few scattered attempts at real mixed bands began along 52nd Street. The important thing was that musicians were getting to know each other; there was no longer a fence that kept a white culture on one side and a Negro culture on the other.

Despite this free exchange of ideas, by the end of the 1930's it began to seem as though a stalemate had been reached. At least, it seemed that way to a small group of musicians, a group who saw jazz from a new perspective. They realized that rhythmically, melodically and harmonically, jazz was in a billion-dollar rut. All the ingenuity of the swing arrangers and soloists could not conceal the fact that the whole gigantic world of jazz, with its millions of notes played nightly by thousands of musicians all over the world, was based entirely on the twelve musical notes of the chromatic scale. The uses to which those twelve notes could be put were in turn limited by the fact that jazz was built entirely on the major, minor, seventh and minor seventh chords based on each of these twel.e notes, plus the diminished and augmented chords, an occasional major seventh and a few other slight variations. Rhythmically, jazz was fundamentally the same mixture of simple syncopations, frequent dotted-eight-and-sixteenth patterns, with the underlying steady four-beats-to-the-bar rhythm section.

How these limitations were bypassed will be explained later in the technical section. What we're concerned with at the moment is the fact that gradually, spontaneously, in various parts of the country, there were a few jazzmen who were finding ways out of this musical straitjacket.

No one musician did it. Dizzy Gillespie did not create bebop in Philadelphia, any more than Charlie Parker created it in Kansas City or Charlie Christian in Oklahoma or Lester Young on the road with Count Basie. What is known today as bebop is a synthesis of many ideas, the product of many original musical minds. In many cases the musicians were not even conscious that they were doing anything startlingly new. Some of them, as far as they were aware, had been playing pretty much the same way all their lives; it was only after they had been in the profession for many years that they found their practice of doing what comes naturally had been branded as a new music and given the name "bebop."

To some of these musicians the heralding of the "new music" seemed a little ironical, since only a few years earlier the same musicians, playing the same music, had been branded as outlaws, rebels or just plain nuts.

Probably the first musician to develop, and place before the public, some of the qualities that later developed into bebop, was the tenor saxophonist Lester Young. Known today as "Pres", the president of the tenor sax men, Lester was first heard of when he replaced Coleman Hawkins in the Fletcher Henderson band in 1934. Hawkins, who had left for Europe after more than a decade with the Henderson band, practically had the tenor sax field to himself; his tone was big, his style forceful and rhythmic. By comparison, Lester Young sounded pale and listless. He did not last long in the Fletcher Henderson band. After joining Count Basie in 1936, however, he leapt into prominence with a record session for Vocalion featuring a quintet out of the Basie band. *Boogie Woogie, Lady Be Good, Evenin'* and *Shoeshine Boy* were Lester's introduction to the record-buying jazz public, and before long he had waxed other solos with the Basie band on Decca, and was impressing fans who heard him on personal appearances with the Count.

Lester was a radical in that he symbolized the gradual evolution from hot jazz to "cool" jazz. To those who measured the value of a jazz improvisation by its degree of superficial intensity or "hotness," Lester's relationship with jazz seemed strangely platonic. His tone sounded dull and flat when contrasted with the big, rich sound of Hawkins' horn; his phrasing seemed slow and lethargic. What became apparent to those who learned to appreciate and respect Lester's originality was that he was rejecting the harshness and blatancy of the earlier jazz in favor of a new relaxation and restraint.

During 1937 and the following two or three years, Lester was heard frequently with various recording combinations assembled by Teddy Wilson, Billie Holiday and others. It is significant that his solos on these old Brunswick and Vocalion sides are acceptable to the ears of today's young jazzmen while so much else on the same records, especially the chugging rhythm sections, has become dated.

Around the same time that Lester was dividing the tenor sax men into two clearly defined schools of Young followers and Hawkins fans, another new star was developing. Charlie Christian, born in Texas and raised in Oklahoma City, started playing the electric guitar in 1937, when he was eighteen. Musicians who heard him around Oklahoma with a band led by Anna Mae Winburn, who later became conductor of the Sweethearts of Rhythm, recall the brilliance and originality of his work.

In 1938 Charlie played for a while in Bismarck, N. D. with a sextet led by pianist Al Trent. Musicians throughout North Dakota and neighboring states were already raving about Christian. A seventeen-year-old girl in Bismarck, Mary Osborne, heard the reports about him and went to the Dome, a dismal spot where the Trent group was working. When she walked in, the sound that greeted her seemed at first to be a tenor sax played through a microphone that distorted the sound a little.

A glance at the bandstand revealed that the soloist was playing a guitar. At that time amplified guitars were a rarity, and the single-note solo style was a complete departure from the pattern of solos in chords established by Carl Kress, Dick McDonough and the other conventional jazz guitarists.

The Trent group had a trumpet, tenor sax, piano, bass, drums, and Christian —but, remarkably, Charlie did not count as a fourth rhythm instrument; rather, he was a third horn, blending the guitar with the tenor and trumpet for three-part voicings that produced a sound new to jazz.

"What impressed everyone most of all," Mary Osborne recalls, "was his sense of time. He had a relaxed, even beat that would sound modern even today. The sextet was doing everything that Benny Goodman did later, and doing it even better. I remember some of the figures Charlie played in his solos—they were exactly the same things that Benny recorded later on as *Flying Home, Gone with What Wind, Seven Come Eleven* and all the others. Charlie didn't play bop exactly, although he did things with augmented and diminished chords that were completely new to me. And rhythmically, some of his ideas sounded very much like bop."

While Christian was working at the Dome, visiting bandleaders tried to lure him away; even Henry Busse offered him a job, but Charlie refused, feeling that he would be better off in obscurity playing the kind of music he liked. In addition to creating his own themes, he would improvise on some of the popular songs that happened to have interesting chord patterns, such as *You Go To My Head* and *My Old Flame*. Occasionally he would even play a Django Reinhardt solo taken note for note from a Reinhardt record. Though the French gypsy's conception of jazz was infinitely removed from Charlie's, he would get a kick out of imitating Django's choruses on *St. Louis Blues* and then following it with something of his own.

The local music shop, aware of the stature Charlie was gaining locally, advertised an electric guitar in its window "As Featured by Charlie Christian at the Dome." When Mary Osborne bought one, and began sitting in with Charlie, he would take a chorus and then, in his gentle, reserved manner, encourage her to follow him.

In July 1939, after John Hammond heard Charlie in Oklahoma City and arranged for him to join Benny Goodman in New York, he came to the attention of some other jazzmen who had been experimenting with new sounds and new ideas. After his job with Benny every evening at the Pennsylvania Hotel, Charlie

6

would take his amplifier and instrument up to a dining room in the Hotel Cecil on West 118th Street in Harlem. Henry Minton, a former saxophonist who had been the first Negro delegate in Local 802, converted the dilapidated room into a club, installed Teddy Hill as manager and made the place an open house for musicians, where jam sessions were practically a nightly event.

Still a bashful, polite small town boy, Charlie soon made many friends and admirers uptown. Jerry Newman, a young jazz fan who used to bring his portable recording machine up to Minton's, recalls that "Charlie never disappointed his listeners, and if he knew that people were paying attention he really improvised. Saturday at Minton's, however, was pretty hectic, with about fifteen men on a small bandstand, all trying to get in their thirty-two bars. When this happened, Charlie would just sit and play chord accompaniments, refusing to take a solo, because he knew it would be wasted. On the few occasions when he felt relaxed, the paying customers paid tribute by standing still in front of the stand and just listening while Charlie played the same exciting jazz that was driving the whole Goodman band."

Some of those moments were captured by Newman on a series of records which he issued many years later in an album on Vox records. They are of more than mere historical interest, since they show the very informal but unmistakable birth pangs of bebop.

Kenny Clarke, who was playing drums at Minton's, declares that "Charlie contributed an infinite amount to the new jazz. He was always very firm about a beat, and we made it our business to swing all the time. He wrote some wonderful tunes, too. One of them was *Paging Dr. Christian;* the first four bars were exactly the same as the number Woody Herman recorded seven years later under the title *Keen and Peachy.* Another one was *Chunk Charlie Chunk;* Jimmy Mundy arranged it and Charlie recorded it with the whole Goodman band as *Solo Flight.*

"One night Charlie and I were at the Douglas Hotel on St. Nicholas Avenue, visiting a friend who was a dancer and played the ukulele. I fooled around with the uke and then Charlie took it out of my hand. 'Look, Kenny,' he said, 'you can make all the chords you want to on this if you just stretch your fingers right.' He showed me, handed back the uke, and I started experimenting. I got an idea that sounded good; went upstairs to my room in the same hotel, and wrote it down. Later on Joe Guy showed the tune to Cootie Williams, and Cootie had Bob MacRae make an arrangement. I called it *Fly Right,* and Cootie used to broadcast it from the Savoy Ballroom. This was right after he'd left Benny Goodman and formed his own band. Cootie recorded it for Columbia but it was never released. Later on I recorded it for Victor with a band of my own under the new title—*Epistrophy.*"

7

Kenny, who had worked with Dizzy in the Teddy Hill band, was a main figure in the group of remnants from the disbanded Hill personnel that went into Minton's in 1940. His theory is that Charlie Christian started the use of the word "bebop." "Charlie and Diz used to hum that way, to illustrate some of their ideas," he recalls.

It was in the Teddy Hill band, Clarke says, that he first began to get away from the steady four-four drumming. "On an arrangement of *Swanee River*, I began kicking, playing off-rhythms. Diz was fascinated; it gave him just the impetus he wanted, and he began to build things around it."

Later, in Minton's as Kenny developed the idea of using the bass drum pedal for special accents rather than regular rhythm, and the top cymbal to maintain the steady four beats, Teddy Hill would imitate the sounds he produced. "What is that kloop-mop stuff you're doing?" he'd say. That's how it sounded to him—Kloop-mop!—and that's what they called the music itself before it became known as bebop, says Hill. In fact, Kenny acquired the nickname of "Kloop," by which he is still known to Minton veterans. Kenny sometimes doubled on vibes; on these occasions Kansas Fields or Jack Parker might sit in on drums, and Kenny's cousin, Sonny White, sometimes took over the piano.

Although Minton's was the focal point of jazz experimentation from 1940 on, its main function was to bring together the men who had been producing new ideas independently, and to help them crystallize these ideas into a new music. One of the youngsters who impressed Clarke most at the time was Tadd Dameron. "I heard Tadd playing flatted fifths in 1940," he remembers. "It sounded very odd to me at first. Tadd was one of the first men I heard playing eighth-note sequences in the new legato manner, too."

The development of these new technical characteristics will be discussed more fully in the second section; meanwhile, it can be stated generally that these musicians began to use notes which, theoretically, just didn't belong in the chord under consideration.

Tadd Dameron, today one of the most famous of bop arrangers, was an early believer in these harmonic departures. Playing his first professional jobs in 1938 with small bands and accompanying vocalists around Ohio, he played chords that few listeners liked or understood. Developing the same ideas in 1939 in Kansas City with Charlie Parker, he heard people say "They're crazy." But when Dizzy Gillespie heard Tadd at a jam session a couple of years later, Diz said— "I've been looking all over for a guy like you."

It was during the Minton's era that men like Dizzy, Clarke and Tadd, finding that to a great degree they were kindred spirits, started what became in effect a

8

clique of new musicians. It was not difficult to prevent outsiders from crashing this charmed circle. As Kenny Clarke recalls, "We'd play *Epistrophy* or *I've Got My Love To Keep Me Warm* just to keep the other guys off the stand, because we knew they couldn't make those chord changes. We kept the riff-raff out and built our clique on new chords."

It was Dizzy who took a popular Hit Parade song of 1940 called *How High The Moon* and changed it from a slow ballad to a jump-tempo instrumental. *How High,* which has since become the virtual national anthem of bebop, and certainly the most-recorded jazz tune of the decade, was actually born in September 1939 when Morgan Lewis, a University of Michigan graduate who had contributed to the scores of a couple of *Little Shows* and a *New Faces,* sat at the piano one day and produced a chord sequence that pleased him. The song was staged by Murray Anderson in *Two For The Show* in the winter of 1940, with Alfred Drake singing Nancy Hamilton's lyrics. The publisher decided to plug the song; it got up to fourth place on the Hit Parade, then disappeared. It was not until the new jazz clique happened to seize on it as a vehicle for improvisation that it began its new and far more prosperous life.

The story of *How High The Moon* illustrates how incongruously the worlds of popular music and jazz sometimes provide each other with inspiration. At one time it was considered corny and "commercial" to use popular songs as a basis for jazz improvisation. Some jazz musicians, and a large number of jazz fans and critics, believed that it destroyed the authenticity of jazz to use anything but the traditional *Tiger Rags* and ragtime standard songs for ad libbing purposes. Actually, of course, jazz has always been inextricably tied up with popular songs to some extent, and even in the early 1920's such numbers as *Dinah* and *Margie* were used by many pioneer jazzmen. Later, jazz artists turned more and more frequently to the Gershwins, the Cole Porters, and even to the less distinguished Tin Pan Alley sources, for new chord patterns. The bebop pioneers were acutely aware of the limitations of *Honeysuckle Rose,* the blues, and the other stale formulae. Though the latter are still used, the boppers like a *Lover Come Back to Me,* or a *Cherokee* for contrast and harmonic variety.

This does not mean that jazzmen are obliged to turn to Tin Pan Alley for musical ideas. On the contrary, Tin Pan Alley has based many of its most successful tunes on musical phrases that were born spontaneously at a jazz session. But if some particular tune which he has heard on the air happens to strike a musician as a good foundation for jazz improvisation, he will use it to build a new and inspired creation of his own, which will often bear no relationship to the original tune melodically, and may even change it harmonically. In many cases the tunes

9

thus used, having acquired new melodies, are given new titles and become separate entities. (A table of examples of this process will be found in the technical section.)

If the jazzmen did not happen to have any contact with the world of popular songs, they would certainly not be at a loss for thematic ideas. At the same period when they were borrowing *How High The Moon* and other hit tunes, the men around Minton's were composing harmonic and melodic structures of their own. Some of them were simple jump tunes based on a repeated riff; others were harmonic departures like *Epistrophy;* a few were slow-tempo, "pretty" tunes with unusual chord changes.

In the last category was *'Round Midnight,* written by Thelonious Monk, a pianist who frequented Minton's. Monk's place in the jazz scene, according to most musicians in the bop movement, has been grossly distorted, as a result of some high-powered publicity work. He has written a few attractive tunes, but his lack of technique and continuity prevented him from accomplishing much as a pianist. In fact, Cootie Williams' original 1944 recording of *'Round Midnight,* arranged for a big band, is vastly superior to Monk's own recording as an interpretation of the theme. Monk, who has been touted as a "genius" and a "high priest of bebop," would wander in and out of Minton's, often falling asleep at the piano. "He'd stay there for hours after the place closed," says Teddy Hill, "or get there hours before we opened. Sometimes the musicians would appeal to me to see if I could wake him up. Suddenly he might wake up and go into some intricate, tricky little passage, with Kenny Clarke playing those funny off-beat effects on the bass drum."

Monk, like all the other musicians who contributed to what eventually became bebop, is an original thinker who undoubtedly contributed to the developments at Minton's, but it cannot be too strongly emphasized, for the benefit of those who hear him in person or on records, that he is not a bebop pianist, nor do his solos have any of the mystic qualities attributed to them by some non-musical admirers. Indeed, Kenny Clarke recalls that Earl (Bud) Powell, a young pianist who was with Cootie's band at the time *'Round Midnight* was recorded, "used to do all the things that Monk wanted to do but couldn't. Bud had more technique; Monk was a teacher, a creator rather than a soloist."

The musicians who saw the birth of the new jazz are almost unanimous on the matter of where the credit belongs for its inception. Virtually everyone mentions Charlie Christian and Lester Young; Dizzy and Tadd Dameron and Kenny Clarke; but without exception, the young musicians today, the jazzmen who believe in modern music and appreciate the art of improvisation, pay tribute to the man they consider a real genius, the living legend of our time—Charlie "Yardbird" Parker.

LAUGHING BOY GILLESPIE, 1944

February 8, 1947: DIZ was one of the first to visit LOUIS ARMSTRONG backstage during Louis' first Carnegie Hall concert. Contrary to publicity stories, they are good friends.

Dizzy and the author (above) with Miss Sweden, Elsie Carlson, examining the manuscript of Dizzy's "Swedish Suite" before its Carnegie Hall premiere; and (below) with Milt Shaw, just before the band sailed for Sweden, January 16, 1948.

CHARLES CHRISTOPHER PARKER, JUNIOR

"I was six years old then," says CHARLIE. "I
a *clean* little bird; lots of things I didn't kr
. . . wish I'd never found them out."

CHARLIE was playing tenor sax with Earl
Hines in 1943. *Courtesy of Benny Harris.*

JAY McSHANN (seated) with BIRD and WALTER BROWN in Dallas, Texas, 1939.

Jay McShann's reed section at the Savoy Ballroom, 1941. Left to right: BOB MABANE, CHARLIE PARKER, JOHN JACKSON, FREDDY CULLIVER.

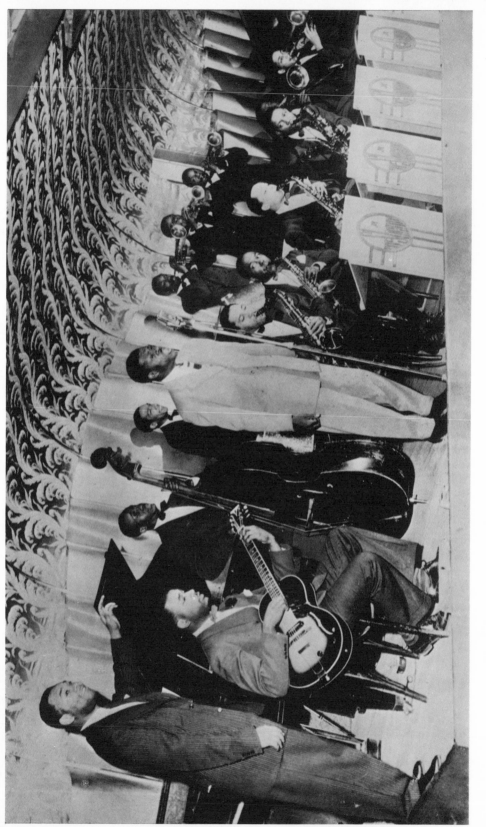

Bird looks up at blues singer WALTER BROWN with the Jay McShann band

Chapter II

Charlie Parker was born in Kansas City, August 29, 1920. As far back as he can remember, he was surrounded by great music in a city that has given jazz so many of its leading stars. A colorful picture of Kansas City night life in the Pendergast era of the 1920's and early 30's can be found in Dave Dexter's book *Jazz Cavalcade* (Chapter 6, "Jazz in the West").

Charlie says that he "spent three years in high school and wound up a freshman." He played baritone horn in the school band and started seriously on alto sax at the age of fifteen, when his mother bought him a horn.

Charlie first went to work for Jay McShann when the band came to Kansas City in 1937, later leaving and rejoining a couple of times. He gained some of his other early experience locally with the bands of Lawrence Keyes and Harlan Leonard.

As early as 1938 Budd Johnson remembers seeing him wander into a Chicago dance hall one night, "looking beat," and without a horn. He wanted to sit in with King Kolax's band. The alto man loaned him one, and when he heard the amazing results, told Charlie that since he happened to have an extra horn and Charlie had none, it would be all right for him to keep this one.

Charlie was without a horn again, though, the following year when he visited New York. Although he stayed around town for several months, he did not work as a musician, and it was not until he made another trip East with McShann that Manhattan musicians had their first chance to hear him.

During McShann's first visit to New York, Charlie met Dizzy Gillespie when Diz sat in with the band one night at the Savoy Ballroom. The Savoy, once regarded as a jazz mecca and nicknamed "the home of happy·feet," was the New York *pied-à-terre* of such bands as Teddy Hill's, Benny Carter's and the late Chick Webb's great swing group in the late 1930's. Savoy audiences consisted of local jitterbugs, who wanted music that jumped, and jazz hunters from downtown, who were concerned more with the esthetic qualities of the performances.

McShann's music, though it had some of the intangible qualities described as "the midwestern beat," conformed pretty closely with the requirements of the Savoy audiences. It was primarily a blues band, featuring one of the better blues shouters of the day, Walter Brown. The arrangements and the solos were generally based on the traditional blues pattern and other simple forms. Charlie Parker wrote a few numbers in this style and played solos on some of the band's first

11

recordings, made in 1941 and '42. His work at that time, as typfied by the recordings of *Hootie Blues* and *Sepian Stomp,* had certain qualities that lifted it above the level of its surroundings. The phrasing was more involved, the tone a little more strident, and the pulse of each performance had a manner of swing that seemed to owe nothing to any source. His use of grace notes and certain dynamic inflections were different from anything that had been heard on the alto, or on any other instrument.

"Charlie Parker offers inspired alto solos," wrote Bob Locke in the July 1, 1942 *Down Beat,* "using a minimum of notes in a fluid style with a somewhat thin tone but a wealth of pleasing ideas." Barry Ulanov, giving the McShann band a rave review in *Metronome,* concurred on Charlie's tone, but instead of "a minimum of notes" he found that the otherwise "superb" "Bird" had a tendency to play too many! In view of the wide variations in his solos at that time it's quite possible that both reviewers were right.

The foundations of Bird's ultimate style were clearly defined before he left Kansas City, but it was in New York that he began experimenting with new harmonic ideas. "I used to hang around with a guitarist named Biddy Fleet," Charlie recalls. "We used to sit in the back room at Dan Wall's chili joint and other spots uptown, and Biddy would run new chords. For instance, we'd find that you could play a relative major, using the right inversions, against a seventh chord, and we played around with flatted fifths. After I left McShann in Detroit and came back to New York, I used to sit in at Minton's with men like Scotty [Kermit Scott, tenor sax], John Simmons on bass, Kenny Clarke or Kansas Fields on drums, and Monk. Those were the guys who'd play everything on the *right* chords—the new chords that we believed were right; and instead of the old tunes we'd play *Cherokee* and *All the Things You Are* and *Nice Work if You Can Get it. . . .*

"But there were some men in McShann's band who'd been developing new ideas, too, especially Johnny Jackson, the other alto man, and Jimmy Forrest on tenor."

Despite Charlie's assertion regarding his colleagues in the McShann band, there was little room for expansion within the harmonic confines of that spirited traditional-styled group. It was when he was playing with a small group at Clark Monroe's Uptown House in Harlem that the New York musicians began to talk about Bird. At that time, according to Kenny Clarke, he was playing alto somewhat in the manner that Lester Young played tenor.

Although his style was evolving into something entirely personal, Charlie did not acquire a real reputation until a couple of years later. He worked on a

12

variety of jobs, even spending nine months working for Noble Sissle, whose band has always been further removed from jazz, and closer to the Broadway commercial concept of dance music, than any other Negro orchestra.

"Sissle hated me," says Charlie, "and I only had one featured number in the books. I doubled on clarinet for that job." Clarinet is by no means Charlie's only double; from time to time he has been heard experimenting with practically every brass and woodwind instrument. Strangely enough, in Earl Hines' orchestra, the first big band in which a bebop clique developed, Charlie played tenor sax.

Earl had originally tried to hire Charlie for an alto chair, early in 1942, under pressure from Scoops Carey, Little Benny and others in the band; but Hines felt badly about taking Bird away from a fellow pianist-maestro, Jay McShann. Calling McShann long distance to give him fair warning that he had musical designs on Parker, he was greeted, to his amazement, with McShann's gleeful answer, "The sooner you take him the better. He just passed out in front of the microphone right in the middle of *Cherokee!*"

It was not until early 1943, when Bird was out of work, that he finally joined Earl. At that time there was no alto chair available, so Earl bought him a tenor and Charlie replaced Budd Johnson.

By now Hines' band was slowly becoming a nursery of new ideas. Earl, though one of the old school himself, encouraged the experimentation that was taking place in the ranks, and gave the boys a free hand. Even Billy Eckstine, who had nothing to do between vocals, studied trumpet as a sideline and picked up some of the ideas traded by Dizzy, Benny, Bird and the rest.

It will always be one of the great regrets of bebop historians that the Hines band of the late 1942 to early 1944 era never made any records, owing to the first recording ban, which went into effect August 1, 1942. It was the first joint engagement of Dizzy and Bird, and a decisive phase in the development of the new music.

After almost a year with Earl, Charlie worked briefly with Cootie Williams and Andy Kirk, then went on the road with the original Billy Eckstine band, in 1944. After leaving Eckstine he was in and out of Fifty Second Street, with Ben Webster, with Dizzy's small band, then with his own group at the Three Deuces featuring an eighteen-year-old trumpeter named Miles Davis. He rejoined Dizzy to go to California and remained there after Dizzy returned East.

Shortly afterwards Charlie went into the physical and mental decline that has become legendary in jazz history. Since he made no bones about it, discussing it frankly when he told me the story for an interview in *Metronome* after his

13

return to New York in 1947, it can be summarized here. Charlie was introduced to night life at its most lurid when he was still an immature lad of about fifteen. Basically he was not, and is not, anti-social or morally bankrupt, but his true character was warped by contact with vicious elements in the Kansas City underworld, and his entire adult life and professional career have been colored both by these contacts and by his background of insecurity and racial discrimination.

Charlie spent many years fighting an addiction which was wrecking his career. In his own words, it took eleven years out of his life. "I didn't know what hit me. . . . I was a victim of circumstances; high school kids don't know any better. That way, you can miss the most important years of your life, the years of possible creation.

"I don't know how I made it through those years. I became bitter, hard, cold. I was always on a panic—couldn't buy clothes or a good place to live. Finally on the Coast I didn't have any place to stay, until somebody put me up in a converted garage. The mental strain was getting worse all the time. What made it worst of all was that nobody understood our kind of music out on the Coast. I can't begin to tell you how I yearned for New York."

The climax came one night at a recording session arranged by Ross Russell, a jazz enthusiast who had started a new company, Dial Records, devoted to bebop. The events at that session and the agonizing weeks that preceded it were graphically described in a fictionalized short story by Elliott Grennard, first published in Harper's magazine and later reprinted in *Prize Stories of 1948* after it had won an O. Henry Memorial Award. Titled "Sparrow's Last Jump," and clearly based on Parker's history, it told of the recordings made by a saxophonist named Sparrow Jones.

The record of *Lover Man* which Charlie made that night was released by Dial. His solo starts a couple of bars late and continues incoherently; it sounds like a shadow of the real Parker. Charlie was unable to finish the session. Later that night he broke down completely. Through the intercession of Ross Russell, he was sent to Camarillo State Hospital, where he remained for seven months. One of his first recordings after his return to the music world was *Relaxing at Camarillo*. It was a typical example of the old Parker brilliance. Charlie soon returned to New York and reconquered Fifty Second Street. Since then, he has worked at the Royal Roost with an all-star group, toured with Norman Granz's "Jazz at the Philharmonic" unit, and made numerous records for Dial and Savoy.

Charlie's evolution as a modern jazzman cannot be ascribed to any one influence. During his first years around jazz, he listened to Herschel Evans and Lester Young, both with Basie; to the late Chu Berry, and to Andy Kirk's tenor

14

man, the late Dick Wilson. He admired Johnny Hodges, Willie Smith and Benny Carter, and especially an alto player named Buster Smith, who did most of the arranging for Count Basie's original band in Kansas City. "I used to quit every job to go with Buster," says Charlie. "But when I came to New York and went to Monroe's, I began to listen to that real advanced New York style. I think the music of today is a sort of combination of the midwestern beat and the fast New York tempos. At Monroe's I heard sessions with a pianist named Allen Tinney; I'd listen to trumpet men like Lips Page, Roy, Dizzy and Charlie Shavers outblowing each other all night long. And Don Byas was there, playing everything there was to be played. I heard a trumpet man named Vic Coulsen playing things I'd never heard. Vic had the regular band at Monroe's, with George Treadwell also on trumpet, and a tenor man named Pritchett. That was the kind of music that caused me to quit McShann and stay in New York."

Like so many modern jazz musicians, Charlie has listened intently to music outside the world of jazz; he has studied Schoenberg, admired Debussy's *Children's Corner*, Stravinsky and Shostakovitch. He credits Thelonious Monk with many of the harmonic ideas that were incorporated into bebop. But he dislikes having any branch of music branded with a name like "bebop." "Let's call it music. People got so used to hearing jazz for so many years; finally somebody said 'Let's have something different' and some new ideas began to evolve. Then people brand it 'bebop' and try to crush it. If it should ever become completely accepted, people should remember it's in just the same position jazz was. It's just another style. I don't think any one person invented it. I was playing the same style years before I came to New York. I never consciously changed my style."

To this it should be added, of course, that Charlie's style did change and mature, though unconsciously, after he came to New York. Like any great jazz musician, he strives constantly for freshness and originality. Moreover, it was not until he started recording with small bands in 1944 that he began to write original compositions in the new style. Even while he was with Hines, he did no writing. According to his recollection, the first arrangers to contribute to the Hines library in the modern style were Dizzy, trombonist Jerry Valentine, and a young trumpeter named Neal Hefti, from Charlie Barnet's band.

Charlie Parker has brought the art of jazz improvisation to a new peak of maturity. A full appreciation of his genius can only be gained by lengthy study of his work both in person and on records. Because of his personal problems, there have been times when he has played without continuity, without inspiration, and even out of tune. Like any other saxophone player, he can be the servant of his horn, and if he has a bad reed, he will squeak like anyone else. These qualifications are not made in an attempt to apologize for Parker's occasional imperfections; they

15

are simply an explanation to the newcomer, who may be confused into interpreting his mistakes as strokes of genius, as do some of the naive young alto sax tyros who copy every note on his record of *Lover Man,* which he wishes had never been released.

Bird's mind and fingers work with incredible speed. He can imply four chord changes in a melodic pattern where another musician would have trouble inserting two. His conception and execution bring to mind Tadd Dameron's comparison of the new jazz with the old: "It's as if you had two roads, both going in the same direction, but one of them was straight with no scenery around it, and the other twisted and turned and had a lot of beautiful trees on all sides."

Charlie Parker takes you along that second road, often at such a speed that at first you may be too dazed to see the view clearly. But speed is not an essential component of his style. On his Dial record of *Embraceable You* he offers a typical Parker treatment of a slow, pretty tune; long, complicated phrases relieved by short, simple ones; sharply contrasted staccato and legato notes; an oblique, devious approach to the harmonic pattern of the tune and an occasional suggestion of the original melody; and always that bitter, caustic yet beautiful tone, a beauty so different from the luxuriant, opulent sound of a lush Johnny Hodges solo that it's hard to believe they both play the same instrument, though Hodges' work has a musical validity of its own and Parker is one of his greatest admirers.

Fortunately it is possible to trace Charlie Parker's career on records without much difficulty; of all the recordings he has made, only those cut with McShann are virtually impossible to obtain. Recorded for Decca's defunct 35 cent label, they may be out soon on Coral.

Following is a discography of Charlie Parker, from which I have excluded records on which he played but did not take any solos.

JAY McSHANN (Decca). The first session was made in New York on April 30, 1941. There is an excellent blues chorus by Charlie on *Hootie Blues* (this composition is credited to Parker and McShann); *Dexter Blues* features an alto solo in conventional blues style not typical of Charlie. On July 2, 1942, Charlie took solos on *The Jumpin' Blues, Sepian Bounce* and *Lonely Boy Blues.*

TINY GRIMES (Savoy). Charlie's first small-band date, September 15, 1944, with the late Clyde Hart, piano; Tiny Grimes, guitar; Hal West, drums, and Jimmy Butts, bass. Originally issued as Tiny Grimes Quintet, then reissued under Parker's name. *Romance Without Finance is a Nuisance* and *I'll Always Love You Just the Same* have Grimes vocals but include great Parker solos; *Tiny's Tempo* is a jump blues instrumental, and *Red Cross* a Parker original.

16

CLYDE HART'S ALL STARS (Continental). Early 1945. *That's The Blues* and *What's The Matter Now* are vocals by Rubberlegs Williams, but with fine backgrounds and solos by Bird, Dizzy, Trummy Young, Don Byas, and rhythm by Hart, Mike Bryan, Al Hall and Specs Powell. *4-F Blues* and *I Want Every Bit of It* were released under Rubberlegs Williams' name, with the same line-up; *Sorta Kinda* and *Seventh Avenue,* with vocals by Trummy, were released under Trummy's name, *Dream of You* and *Ooh! Ooh! My! My!* also have Trummy vocals but are listed under Dizzy.

DIZZY GILLESPIE (Guild). Reissued on Musicraft. First date, February 28, 1945: *Groovin' High, Dizzy Atmosphere* and *All the Things You Are,* with Clyde Hart, Remo Palmieri, Slam Stewart and Cozy Cole. Second date May 11, 1945: Dizzy, Bird, Al Haig, Curly Russell, Sid Catlett in *Shaw Nuff* (Bird's tune), *Salt Peanuts, Hot House* and *Lover Man* (last side features Sarah Vaughan).

SARAH VAUGHAN (Continental). May 25, 1945. On the second of two sessions we assembled for Sarah, Bird was in the band along with Dizzy, Flip Phillips, the late Nat Jaffe on piano, Curly Russell and Max Roach. Solo by Bird on *Mean To Me;* backgrounds only on *What More Can a Woman Do* and *I'd Rather Have a Memory.*

RED NORVO (Comet). June 5, 1945. Dizzy, Bird, Flip, Teddy Wilson, Slam; J. C. Heard and Specs Powell splitting the date on drums. Four great twelve-inch sides: *Congo Blues* and *Get Happy; Slam Slam Blues* and *Hallelujah.*

SLIM GAILLARD (Bel-Tone). December, 1945. Reissued on Majestic. Bird, Dizzy and tenor man Jack McVea can be heard talking and playing in the informal *Slim's Jam;* with Slim on guitar, vibes and vocals, Bam Brown on bass and Zutty Singleton on drums, they also took part in *Dizzy Boogie, Popity Pop* and *Flat Foot Floogee,* all interesting for their curiosity and novelty value rather than for the music.

JAZZ AT THE PHILHARMONIC (Disc). Recorded in 1946 by Norman Granz at his jazz concerts. Bird can be heard in Volumes 2 and 6.

SIR CHARLES (Apollo). An all-star session led by pianist Charlie Thompson, with Buck Clayton, Dexter Gordon, Danny Barker, J. C. Heard and Jimmy Butts. Solos by Bird on *Takin' Off, 20th Century Blues* and *The Street Beat.*

CHARLIE PARKER: the first session actually led by Bird was made early in 1945 with Miles Davis on trumpet, Dizzy Gillespie on piano (also doubling on trumpet in the intro and coda of *Ko-Ko,* Curly Russell and Max Roach. Variously labeled as "Charlie Parker's Ri Bop Boys," "Charley Parker's Ree

Boppers" and "The Be Bop Boys," the four sides, all Parker tunes, were *Billie's Bounce, Now's The Time, Ko-Ko* and *Thriving From A Riff.* Bird's concluding ad lib chorus on the last side later became known as a composition in its own right, entitled *Anthropology.*

CHARLIE PARKER SEPTET (Dial). March 28, 1946, in Hollywood, with Miles Davis, Lucky Thompson, Dodo Marmarosa, Arv Garrison, Vic McMillan, and Roy Porter. *Moose the Mooche* and *Yardbird Suite,* Bird's tunes; also Dizzy's *Night in Tunisia* and Benny Harris' *Ornithology.* A different master of the last side was issued separately under the title *Bird Lore.*

CHARLIE PARKER (Dial). July 29, 1946. This was the date described earlier in this chapter. *Lover Man* was released under Parker's name and *Bebop* under Howard McGhee's. With Jimmy Bunn, piano; Bob "Dingbod" Kesterton, bass, Roy Porter, drums.

MILES DAVIS (Savoy). 1947. This unique session features Charlie on tenor sax. John Lewis, piano; Nelson Boyd, bass, and Max Roach. All originals by Miles: *Little Willie Leaps, Half Nelson, Milestones* and *Sipping at Bell's.*

CHARLIE PARKER: All other 1947 records can be found under Charlie's own name on Dial or Savoy. Dial sides recommended are *Bird's Nest,* with Erroll Garner on piano; *Relaxing at Camarillo, Cheers, Carving the Bird* and *Stupendous* (February 27, 1947) with Howard McGhee, Wardell Gray, Dodo, Kessel, Callender and Lamond. Savoy sides include *Cheryl* and the amazing *Bird Gets The Worm,* both in an album called "The Parkers," featuring three sides each by Charlie Parker and Leo Parker. Also on Savoy are *Buzzy* and *Donna Lee,* with Miles, Max Roach, Tommy Potter, and great piano by Bud Powell.

Charlie is featured in an original composition by Neal Hefti, made by a large orchestra with strings, which was recorded for inclusion in a special Norman Granz album of modern music on Mercury.

Chapter III

Although Dizzy Gillespie is by no means the only musician who originated, developed or popularized bebop, it is true that to a large extent the history of Dizzy, at least since 1940, is the history of bebop. He has figured so prominently in every development since that year that the stories of Bird, Monk, Kloop and the others all dovetail into Dizzy's biography. During this chapter, then, after first backtracking to give Dizzy's personal pre-New York background, it will be possible to follow the winding course of bop as we trace Gillespie's own peregrinations.

John Birks Gillespie was the ninth and last child born to Mrs. Lottie Gillespie, and is the only one making his living as a musician. Two children died in infancy; Edward, a brother, died in 1935. Jimmy, the senior brother, is a taxi-driver in New York City; Wesley, a year older than John, is an expert chef at a smart Russian restaurant in Philadelphia. Mattie, oldest of the surviving six children, and her sister Eugenia, live with their mother in a somber apartment one flight up at 1342 Catharine Street in Philadelphia.

Although Dizzy's father was a bricklayer, music was a main phase of activity in the Gillespie household. When Dizzy was born on October 21, 1917 in the small South Carolina town of Cheraw, Gillespie, Sr., an amateur musician, led a local band as a sideline, and kept its members' instruments at his home. Dizzy's introduction to music thus equipped him with a working knowledge of several other instruments besides trumpet.

"My father treated my mother good," Dizzy once told Richard Boyer. "He got my mother real expensive stuff. I was scared of him, though. When he talked, he roared. He was a real man. He didn't have a voice like this." Dizzy ended the sentence in a falsetto. "I got a beating every Sunday morning." He exploded into mirth. "At school, I was smart, but I didn't study much. I'd fight every day. Ev-er-y day I'd fight. I was *all*-ways bad, you know."

The elder Gillespie died in 1927, when John was ten. During the next few years his musical interests enabled him to get a scholarship to a Negro industrial school in North Carolina, the Laurinburg Institute. He started on trombone at fourteen, taking music seriously for the first time. Nine months later a neighbor, James Harrington, loaned him a trumpet, and not long after that he was given a trumpet of his own at Laurinburg, where an instructor whose name he recalls as Shorty Hall taught him theory and harmony.

19

Dizzy never studied trumpet at school. Nor did he become an expert reader until many years later. However, he soon mastered the horn well enough to play with a ten piece band of youngsters, featuring such early swing arrangements as the Casa Loma Orchestra's *Wild Goose Chase*.

When Dizzy's mother left Cheraw in 1935 to live in Philadelphia, he had to quit school several months before his class graduated. Not until he visited Laurinburg in 1947 for a special ceremony did he receive his diploma and football letter.

Arriving in Philly with his trumpet in a paper bag, John Gillespie was still a rough and rowdy country boy, his hat cocked on one side and a smart-alecky manner to match. Contrary to many subsequent claims of origination by Teddy Hill and others, it was around this time that he acquired the nickname of Dizzy.

Charlie Shavers and Carl "Bama" Warwick were the other trumpet men in the local band led by Frank Fairfax which gave Dizzy his first important job. Dizzy, listening to Teddy Hill's band broadcasting from the Savoy Ballroom over NBC, had found a musical idol in Hill's star trumpet man, Roy Eldridge, and was playing in a style approximating Roy's.

Dizzy's next job ended before it started; Lucky Millinder heard him and hired him, but after Diz had left town to join Lucky, something went wrong and he wound up in New York without a job. However, providence was on hand in the person of Teddy Hill, whose trumpet ace had left to join Fletcher Henderson in Chicago. Frankie Newton was holding down the chair, but Teddy was looking for someone who could play like Roy. Having once heard Dizzy in Philadelphia, he invited him to come to a rehearsal. The brass section had been called to rehearse an hour or two before the reeds.

Bill Dillard, later to make a name for himself as an actor, was playing first trumpet, and Shad Collins was on second. Teddy switched Shad to third and gave Dizzy the second book. Diz got on the bandstand warmly clothed—overcoat and gloves included—and remained that way throughout the rehearsal. During the subsequent years with Hill, Dizzy studiously avoided any attempt to belie his nickname. Embarking on a new arrangement, he was likely to start it by reading an interlude, or the last chorus, instead of taking it from the top. While somebody else took a solo, Dizzy might stand up in the corner miming, imitating the soloist, holding up his horn and pretending to blow. Often he'd play an extra bar or two at the end of a number, a habit that persists today.

Dizzy would always respond, though hardly in the manner expected, to Teddy Hill's attempts to discipline him. If Teddy reprimanded him for putting his foot upon a chair, he'd remove it promptly—and rest the foot on a music stand.

No less disturbing were such early antics as dancing in the middle of someone else's act, putting the trumpet derby on his head, and playing with his chair turned backwards, facing away from the audience. But by the time Dizzy made his first record session with Hill in March 1937, he had established his musical value to the band. His solos on *King Porter Stomp* and *Blue Rhythm Fantasy* attested to his careful study of Roy Eldridge. Howard Johnson, the lanky, smiling first alto man who was to play in Diz's own band a decade later, encouraged the resemblance by writing out some of Roy's stuff to make it easier for Diz to copy it.

Although some of the men in the band resented Dizzy, Teddy decided to take him along when the possibility of a European tour came up. There was some talk about getting a man with more of a name; a few men even threatened to leave the band if Dizzy were not fired. But Teddy called their bluff, kept Dizzy, and of course the men stayed anyway. The band spent a happy summer in London and Paris, serving as background for a Cotton Club show with the Berry Brothers and several other name acts.

For British jazz fans the Teddy Hill tour marked the first visit of an American band in several years, since the British Ministry of Labor had clamped down on all imported music, and only lifted the ban in this instance with the strict provision that Teddy's men be used strictly as background for the acts.

Seeing the band at the London Palladium, I can remember straining to catch a few bars of trumpet obbligato by Bill Dillard or Shad Collins while the Berry Brothers danced. The unknown third trumpet man, John Gillespie, was of no interest to me or to any of the jazz fans, who were mainly interested in the names they recognized from records, such as Russ Procope, who was playing alto in the band, and Dickie Wells, the trombonist, who subsequently made some great records in Paris featuring a brass contingent from the band—but omitting the unfortunate third trumpeter.

Dizzy was having a happy time, however. Sometimes he'd sit in with the hip little mixed band at London's only after-hours jazz spot, the Nest. On the job with Hill, he'd help to set up ideas for head arrangements, get the brass section to stay behind after rehearsals and work up some stuff. Later on, back in the States, he would set choruses for the production numbers when they played the Apollo and other theatre dates.

The European trip, for Diz, was a chance to see some of the world while he was still in his teens, to see the sights and take pictures, and to indulge in a few eccentricities such as the wearing of a British regimental busby with a strap under the chin—a forerunner of the beret fashion he was to set later.

21

Back in the States, Diz decided to transfer into New York's Local 802, and was thus prevented by union rules from doing any steady work in New York until he had his local card. Filling in the transfer time with odd jobs, he recalls, "I worked with one cat in the Bronx who doubled on bass and musical saw."

After getting his 802 card, Dizzy rejoined Teddy. He was now able to make a steady living, and out of the $45 a week earned at the Savoy by Hill's sidemen, plus a few extras when the band went on one-nighters or theatres, Dizzy somehow managed to save a little and send money to his family in Philly. He even made frequent loans to other men in the band, just to avoid throwing his money away. Dizzy was not the type to use up all his loot on liquor and chicks, despite his other wild characteristics. He was still a kid at heart. Teddy Hill's house was his home away from home, a playground where he could romp with Teddy's little girl, Gwendolyn, telling her that candy wasn't good for her and then eating it all himself.

Before long Dizzy was playing first trumpet with Hill, also taking most of the solos, and the other two men in the section in 1939-40, Al Killian and Joe Guy, were learning from Dizzy rather than teaching him. He helped them with their reading, impressed them with his musical diligence.

He impressed people outside the band, too. One day a young chorus girl at the Howard Theatre in Washington heard him, and that, declares Dizzy, was how he won his wife. Lorraine Willis, a pretty dancer, became his bride in Boston on May 9, 1938. (Possibly Lorraine married him because he was a good cook. Earlier, when she was working at the Apollo and he was idle, awaiting his card, he'd cook elaborate meals and take them to the theatre for her.)

Diz did no more recording until Lionel Hampton roped him in on an all-star small-band date for Victor on September 11, 1939. Diz was the whole brass section, working with a phenomenal sax team comprising Benny Carter on alto, Coleman Hawkins, Ben Webster and the late Chu Berry on tenors. Listed on the labels as "C. Gillespie," Dizzy took one solo—the muted opening chorus on *Hot Mallets*—showing a definite trend away from the Eldridge style and a slight hint of the typical Gillespian cascades of eighth notes that eventually marked his work. ("Dizzy Gillespie, the new colored trumpet find, sells some solid stuff in the first chorus," I wrote in the November 1939 *Swing* Magazine, though who was supposed to have "found" Dizzy or who told me he was a find I can't remember.)

1939 saw Dizzy working at the New York World's Fair, where Teddy Hill was installed in a supposed replica of the Savoy Ballroom. He also worked for a couple of months with Edgar Hayes, a pianist whose schmaltzy record of *Stardust* had made him a Harlem juke box favorite.

22

While he was rehearsing with Hayes, Dizzy heard some effects in an arrangement by the clarinet man, Rudy Powell (later known as Musheed Karweem) that sounded weirdly different. "I played it over and over," he recalled years later, "and realized how much more there could be in music than what everybody was playing." It may well be that this was the beginning of Dizzy's real musical awakening and the expansion of his style. Another important factor was his determination to stop copying Roy, and outblow him by developing a style of his own.

Returning to Teddy Hill briefly, until the band broke up as a result of managerial difficulties, Dizzy landed an assignment that was to be perhaps the pivotal job of his career. Late in 1939 he joined the orchestra of Cab Calloway.

Record collectors who have attempted a complete discography of Dizzy need hardly be told of the important developments that took place in the two years Dizzy spent with Cab. Diz cut some fifty sides with the band for the Vocalion label (later known as Okeh), and although Cab hogs many of them with his vocals, there are numerous examples of the blossoming Gillespie talent.

Pickin' the Cabbage, composed and arranged by Diz, is the best example. A minor key tune in the two-bar riff tradition of the swing era, it nevertheless went far enough within this stale pattern to acquire a personal tone-color and a fine sense of dramatic construction. On the other side of the disc, *Paradiddle,* drummer Cozy Cole was featured in a little "kloop-mop" act he'd worked out with Diz. Between Cozy, Dizzy and Chu Berry, plus the work of such men as Tyree Glenn on trombone and vibes, Jerry Blake on clarinet and Milton Hinton on bass, there was plenty going on in the band besides hi-de-ho.

On *A Bee Gezindt,* a series of unison band vocals introduced some of the soloists. "He's Diz the Whiz, a solid sender, a very close friend of Mrs. Bender," sang the guys, whereupon Diz blew four bars for posterity. He had some longer solos, too, on such sides as *Calling All Bars, Hard Times, Bye Bye Blues, Boo-Wah Boo-Wah* and *Cupid's Nightmare,* the last-named being an early example of how pretty the Gillespie horn can sound on occasion.

The job with Cab came to an abrupt end in September 1941. Cab had accused Dizzy of throwing spitballs at him in the middle of a stage show in Hartford, Conn. There was a scuffle backstage. Diz readily admitted afterwards that he'd been far from blameless. The story made Diz a talked-about name in music circles for the first time, and for the wrong reason.

"Cab Calloway still has a sore rear end," said *Down Beat* delicately in a long news story on the fracas. "Cabell took ten stitches from a doctor."

23

For a few weeks Diz worked with the Ella Fitzgerald band, which Ella had inherited from her boss, the late Chick Webb. His old pal Kenny Clarke, who'd been helping Teddy Hill to establish Minton's, was also with Ella. Diz liked the job, especially when he heard Dick Vance, the lead trumpet man, play a clean altissimo B Flat on the end of an arrangement Diz had just written called *Down Under*. But Diz never got to record this or any other number with Ella, though a few months later he sold *Down Under* to Woody Herman, who cut it for Decca.

By this time, Dizzy was making definite strides as an arranger. He wrote a new minor key opus, slower and more exotic than *Pickin' the Cabbage*. It was used later to feature trombonist Benny Green in the Earl Hines band, and Hines gave it the title *Night In Tunisia*. Dizzy also placed several originals with Jimmy Dorsey and Ina Ray Hutton. But selling arrangements was an arduous and undependable business; much less gratifying, for instance, than settling down on an easy 52nd Street location in a six-piece band, especially when you were working for a wonderful guy like Benny Carter.

It was with Carter that Dizzy played his first jazz concert, at the Museum of Modern Art in November 1941, with Carter's group and Maxine Sullivan co-starred. ("Dizzy Gillespie's trumpeting is top-notch . . . . he fits in excellently with the Carter ensemble," decided Barry Ulanov, covering the sextet for *Metronome*.)

Dizzy's sojourn in the Carter band (which also included Kenny Clarke) was the occasion for my first full-scale introduction to his work in person. At the Famous Door, where the group had a featured spot in the floor show, using an arrangement I'd made for Benny on *Lady Be Good*, the solos were taken by Benny on alto, Al Gibson on clarinet (later replaced by Jimmy Hamilton) and Dizzy. Benny found Dizzy's style alternately fascinating and nerve-wracking, this being an effect he had on many listeners at the time, myself included. In fact, when I had to assemble a small band for a Pete Brown-Helen Humes date on Decca, and was stuck for a trumpet, I was reluctant to use Diz, since this was a blues session and I could hardly see him as a blues man. I finally did use Diz on the date, along with a couple of other men from Carter's group, but didn't give him a solo bar on the whole session. He read the music excellently, but if I'd thrown away my arrangements and let him loose, *Unlucky Woman Blues* and *Mound Bayou* could have become Gillespie collectors' items.

Diz interrupted his stay with Benny to go on the road for a few weeks with Charlie Barnet around the Christmas-New Year's season. Barnet says that in the light of what has happened since then, he realizes that his reaction to Dizzy at that time, which was generally one of impatience at his nonconformity, was due to unfamiliarity with Diz's musical motives. "Dizzy's the greatest," reported Joe Guy some time afterwards. "I was in the Barnet band when he was. He has an extraordinary style—I'd say it was based mostly on augmented chords. . . ." (You'd be wrong, Joe.) "He never gets tired of playing; he'll do sixteen sets and then go across the street and jam with someone else. The other evening Oscar Pettiford and I went to his house about 6:30 a. m., woke him up and started a jam session. And I've spent whole evenings listening to his collection of records—classical and jazz."

After playing the Famous Door and Kelly's Stables for several months, the Carter group broke up in February 1942. Before long he had another big-band job, working for Les Hite. Formerly a popular maestro in California, Hite was making a hazardous Eastern venture with the help of a wealthy backer who was running the band as a somewhat unprofitable hobby. Walter Fuller was writing for the band and there was some good music. The leader and most of his sidemen regarded Diz with a mixture of amusement, irritation and respect. That the respect was justified can be heard clearly in Dizzy's half-chorus on *Jersey Bounce* (Hit Records), probably the first example of pure bebop on records. By now Dizzy's style was clearly formed, his tone excellent and his ideas faster-flowing than ever.

After hours, there was still Minton's Play House—and the Jay McShann band was in town, at the Savoy, which meant that Bird was likely to be around too. ("The jazz set forth by the Parker alto is superb. Parker's tone tends to rubberiness, and he has a tendency to play too many notes, but his continual search for wild ideas, and the consistency with which he finds them, compensate for weaknesses that should be easily overcome." Ulanov, March 1942, *Metronome.*) Monk was still a frequent visitor; Little Benny Harris would drop in when he got through with the job in Pete Brown's group downtown at Kelly's. But Charlie Christian would enliven the sessions no more. Taken to Bellevue the previous July, the great young talent from Texas passed away March 2, 1942, in a Staten Island sanitarium. And not long after, on July 30, another young man, who had done as much for the bass as Christian had for the guitar, was lost to jazz when Jimmy Blanton, also a victim of t.b., passed away.

Dizzy and Bird were still just a couple of unrelated, better-than-average sidemen. Nothing much was happening for Diz around New York; a little work with Lucky Millinder, including a record date (*Are You Ready?* and *When The Lights Go On Again,* not featuring Diz); a job with Calvin Jackson at the Sky Club. Diz decided to go home to Philly, where he formed a quartet at the Down Beat with Johnny Ace, piano, Oscar Smith, bass, and a succession of drummers, one of whom was a local white boy named Stan Levey. New ideas still kept coursing through the Gillespie mind and fingers; sometimes he'd spend as much time at the piano as he did blowing trumpet. The use of flatted fifths in improvisation was already a commonplace with Diz, though to many fellow-musicians they still sounded like wrong notes.

Little Benny was in the Earl Hines band now, and straining to work with some trumpet men who'd give him stiff competition instead of dragging him. Before long Gillespie joined the Fatha.

Although Charlie Parker was in this band, Dizzy paid little attention to him at first. His awareness of Parker's talent came about in a strangely indirect fashion. Little Benny had copied out Bird's alto solo from the McShann record of *Sepian Bounce*. One night with Hines he played it on trumpet, much to Dizzy's delight. "You like that?" said Benny. "Well, it's Bird's." Dizzy soon realized that many other great things were Bird's too. The curious combination of syncopated and on-the-beat figures that later became known as *Mop Mop* was one of Bird's passing fancies. (A little later Kenny Clarke created a full composition based on the phrase, and Coleman Hawkins, who was fronting Clarke's band, copyrighted the tune.)

Dizzy found plenty of musical excitement as the weeks went by in the Hines band. He never tired of playing; one night in Chicago, Diz persuaded Oscar Pettiford to trudge through ten long city blocks in a snowstorm, carrying his bass, to join him in a hotel room for an all-night jam session. Often in New York, up at the Dewey Square, or at Dizzy's apartment nearby, there would be Bud Powell and Benny Harris and Freddy Webster, to whom playing and talking and thinking meant more than eating and drinking.

On April 23, 1943, Hines opened at the Apollo in Harlem. The curtains parted to reveal two pianos. At one sat the Fatha; at the other was a shy young girl from Newark whom Billy Eckstine had recommended to Earl for a vocal spot with the band. Later she left the piano and came front and center to sing *Body and Soul*. This was Sarah Vaughan's debut in the big time, and her first alliance with a group of people who were to play vital parts in her career—Eckstine, Parker and Gillespie.

Sarah's own influence as a musician is not to be discounted. Many were the nights when she would sit around at the piano after the dance was over, working out new ideas. It was for Sarah that Dizzy began to write arrangements in the Hines band, but what he did with *East of the Sun* turned out to be too unusual; it "didn't catch on," says Earl, and they couldn't use the arrangement. (A year later Sarah sang this number with a Dizzy background on her first record date.)

26

DIZZY, aged 17, just before he left Cheraw, S. C.

ILLY ECKSTINE, with trumpet, lead-
g his band at the Tic Toc in Boston,
944, with DIZZY. In background,
ext to BILLY, is LUCKY THOMPSON.

Oscar Pettiford's band at the Onyx Club on West 52nd Street, 1944. Left to right: HAROLD (DOC) WEST, OSCAR PETTIFORD, JOE SPRINGER, JOE GUY, HOT LIPS PAGE (who was working as a single, not with the band) and JOHNNY HARTZFIELD.

The first bop band on 52nd Street, 1944. MAX ROACH, DON BYAS, OSCAR PETTIFORD, GEORGE WALLINGTON, DIZZY. *Courtesy George Wallington.*

DIZZY recorded Jerome Kern's music with a string background in Hollywood, 1945; the records were never released.

Jam session at the Village Vanguard, February 1942. DIZZY, HARRY LIM, VIDO MUSSO, BILLY KYLE, COOTIE WILLIAMS, CHARLIE SHAVERS, and bassist JOHNNY WILLIAMS. *CHARLES PETERSON*

The Hines bubble burst when Billy Eckstine finally moved out. A sensation on every job the band played, Billy had become the real selling point of Earl's organization, though he was still working for a relatively modest weekly salary. By now John Hammond wanted to arrange a solo build-up for Billy; Duke Ellington offered him $300 a week to join the band. Billy Shaw of the William Morris office, Hines' booking agency, didn't want to touch Billy for fear of offending Earl. Finally a call from Count Basie convinced him that Eckstine was too hot to ignore. Hines and Shaw didn't speak for a year after the latter decided to launch Eckstine on a career as a solo singer.

For the Hines band, this was a disaster of such proportions that the only way to compensate was by doing something startlingly different and pretentious. Earl decided on a pseudo-symphonic mixed band, with a girl string section, even a girl bass and guitarist. In September, Paul Cohen, a young white trumpeter, took Dizzy's chair and Dizzy joined Coleman Hawkins.

It was probably just as well that Dizzy came off the road when he did. The summer of 1943 was an eventful period in New York for the new movement of which nobody was yet fully aware. Benny Carter had breezed into town with a new big band featuring a 19-year-old trombonist from Indianapolis—"J. J. Johnson, of whose fine, driving style you will certainly hear more," to quote a gross understatement from my *Metronome* review. Gene Krupa had introduced a 17-year-old pianist from Pittsburgh named Dodo Marmarosa. Charlie Barnet's band brought something new to jazz stage presentation with his bass duet number featuring Chubby Jackson and Oscar Pettiford, both of whom were doing things that hadn't been heard since Blanton's halcyon days. Howard McGhee, who had left Barnet and started his own 12-piecer in Detroit, seemed to be developing along original lines as a modern trumpet stylist.

None of these events, however, seemed to be interrelated in any way, nor did they help Dizzy to rise above the status of an irregularly employed sideman. In October, when Duke Ellington needed to replace three men (Junior Raglin, Nat Jones and Harold Baker) for a date at the Capitol Theatre, because they didn't have Local 802 cards, he hired three men who happened to be unemployed: John Simmons, Toby Hardwick, and Dizzy.

The first week at the Capitol broke an all-time record, a phenomenon due to the presence of Lena Horne as headliner rather than to Dizzy's membership in the band. Ray Nance played, sang and danced; Taft Jordan blew like crazy on *Blue Skies;* Rex Stewart went through his *Boy Meets Horn* routine; but aside from a few background choruses during the dance acts, Dizzy did nothing. Musicians in the band recall that the Ellington-Gillespie alliance was not a particularly happy one all around. Dizzy didn't dig the band's kind of music and the band didn't dig Dizzy. Everyone was glad when the three weeks were over, with the possible exception of Duke himself, who later became one of Dizzy's most distinguished admirers.

By this time the war had brought 52nd Street to a zenith of activity, with as many as five or six spots featuring small jazz groups concurrently: Kelly's, the Onyx, the Three Deuces, the Yacht Club (or Famous Door) and the Spotlite. The music on the street was heterogeneous, featuring neat little arranged groups such as Red Norvo's, an occasional semi-Dixieland unit like Red Allen's, and, by early 1944, a few reflections of the new things that had been happening at Minton's and in the Hines band. With the wartime shortage of manpower affecting even allegedly unhealthy people like musicians, there was keen competition for talent, and often bands had to be formed specially to fill the jobs. In this way Dizzy and Oscar Pettiford had a chance to open with a small group. Oscar wanted Dizzy to be the leader; after an exchange of "No, you" and "Why not you?" it was decided to put both names on the banner outside. With Don Byas on tenor, George Wallington on piano and Max Roach on drums, Diz and Oscar opened, both earning $75 a week while Byas got $60 and the other men union scale, which was around $50.

The money wasn't the greatest, but the music was a real crystallization of all the ideas that had never before found such a regular outlet. All five men thought very much alike, though Don was never exactly a bop musician. New tunes grew out of improvisations so fast that the men had to remind one another to write them down. Oscar had one featuring Roach which he called *Max Is Making Wax* (recorded later by Pettiford with a big band as *Something for You*, on Manor); he featured his own bass work on *Bass Face*, which later came to light in a revised form as *One Bass Hit*, featured by Ray Brown. Diz had a cute little octave-jump riff thing on which, instead of playing the octave jump, he sang "Salt peanuts, salt peanuts!" And he had a minor-key number which, because its main phrase could best be described verbally by repeating the sound *"bebop!"* later came to be given that title. So many of the rhythmic ideas developing at that time seemed to end with a staccato two-note phrase, suggesting the word "bebop," that this onomatopeic term soon began to be applied by the 52nd Street denizens to describe all the music played by Dizzy and his clique. It was thus, late in 1944, that most of us who were around Dizzy and his contemporaries began to be conscious that there was a musical genre sufficiently distinct to have earned a special name. "He plays all that bebop stuff," you would say, or perhaps "rebop," since either sound was equally representative of the musical phrase

28

referred to. Later "rebop" dropped out of fashion, although for some reason it hung on in England, where the bop fans still talk avidly of the "rebop movement."

It was while Dizzy and Oscar were bringing bop to 52nd Street that Coleman Hawkins, working a block away at Kelly's, used them for an historic record session. Hawk, an enthusiast for the new music ever since he had first heard Dizzy, assembled a ten-piece band for a date that set three precedents. In addition to being the first session cut for the new Apollo label, it was the first date Dizzy had made since the lifting of the recording ban, and the first strictly bebop unit ever assembled for records.

Actually it took two nights to make the six sides that resulted. Owing to the inexperience of those in charge of the recording, the unfamiliarity of some of the musicians with the music and their difficulties in reading and interpreting it correctly, the whole thing was a protracted headache for everyone concerned, but the music produced justified all the trouble.

Three of the sides were clearly bop. One was Dizzy's own *Woody'n You,* named for Woody Herman (but never recorded by him) and later retitled *Algo Bueno* when the Gillespie band cut it for Victor. The others were Budd Johnson's *Bu-Dee-Daht* and a blues riff called *Disorder at the Border.* The remaining three sides were mainly tenor solos by Hawkins.

Because of the problems of finding trombonists who could face the fast-moving technical passages involved in the new music (there are precious few good bop trombonists even today), Hawkins' band comprised trumpets, saxes and rhythm. The trumpets were Dizzy, Vic Coulsen and Ed Vanderveer; altos, Leonard Lowry and Leo Parker; tenors, Hawk and Don Byas (Ray Abramson on some sides); baritone, Budd Johnson; piano, Clyde Hart; drums, Max Roach; and bass, Oscar Pettiford.

Budd Johnson, who had switched to baritone for this date, took his place alongside Dizzy and Oscar, playing tenor in the little band at the Onyx, when Don Byas left to join Duke Ellington. (The job with Duke, as it turned out, never materialized.) The music was great at the Onyx, and business was good enough to keep Dizzy and Oscar there for three months.

It was Budd who helped to develop the unison ensemble style that became definitive of small band bebop; he and Oscar suggested that Diz write down some of the things he was doing so that the two horns could play them in unison.

After the Onyx job, when Dizzy and Oscar split up, Diz took Budd and Max with him into a spot right across the street known temporarily as the Yacht

29

Club. Oscar, staying on at the Onyx for 16 more weeks, used Joe Guy in Dizzy's place, Johnny Hartzfield on tenor, Joe Springer on piano and Harold West on drums. Guy, a colleague of Diz on and off since the Teddy Hill and Minton's days, was showing the influence of the new school, and the rest of the new Pettiford group conformed pretty much with the style of its predecessor. Thus there were now two bebop bands on 52nd Street.

Also at the Yacht Club was Billy Eckstine, working as a single and billed, through a brainstorm of Billy Shaw's, as X-Tine. The singer had been laying eggs at the Zanzibar, the Yacht and other spots and Shaw was undecided what to do with him. Finally it was resolved to see if he could be booked as a bandleader, heading a large unit under his own name.

By the time Eckstine started lining up his personnel, Dizzy had closed at the Yacht Club and was filling in time with John Kirby's sextet at the Aquarium on Broadway. (Kirby, who possibly didn't trust Dizzy, had Charlie Shavers come in to make the broadcasts.) Eckstine, who wanted Dizzy to help him form the band and act as its musical director, fought Billy Shaw about the kind of music and musicians to be featured. Disarming Shaw with such statements as "Billy, this is the music of tomorrow and we've got to fight it through!" he went to Chicago to get Gail Brockman, another Hines trumpet section alumnus; Jerry Valentine, the trombonist and arranger; and Charlie Parker, who was then with Carroll Dickerson at the Rhumboogie. Bird played first alto, with Bob Williams in the other alto chair; Dizzy led the trumpet section.

The news that Dizzy was to play such a prominent part in the Eckstine venture did not meet with unanimous rejoicings. The road manager whom Shaw had hired to travel with the band refused the job when he was told the news. "I've heard too much about Dizzy," he declared. Shaw called Diz into his office for a lecture. "If you do well, this'll be your big chance to straighten out. After Eckstine's all set and established, I'll go to work on you and build you with your own band."

Dizzy nodded wisely and gravely. On the band's first date, a theatre booking in Baltimore (June 9, 1944), he overslept on the train and woke up in Washington. He arrived back in Baltimore in time to see the end of the first show.

Eckstine's confidence in the new music proved to be justified. The band, instead of hampering him, seemed to help sell his singing. Moreover, having given up hope of ever catching up with Dizzy on the trumpet, Eckstine had bought a valve trombone and was experimenting with it as a medium for the same style.

So much great talent passed through the Eckstine ranks during the next year that it is still a source of regret among musicians that the band was never recorded. While he was still organizing, Billy cut a date for De Luxe. The recording was so miserable that it is hard to imagine how the band sounded in the studio, with this amazing line-up: Al Killian, Freddy Webster, Shorty McConnell, trumpets; Trummy Young, Howard Scott, Claude Jones, trombones; Budd Johnson, Jimmy Powell, Rudy Rutherford, Wardell Gray, Tommy Crump, saxes; Clyde Hart, Connie Wainright, Oscar Pettiford and Shadow Wilson, rhythm. This group made *I Stay in the Mood For You* and *Good Jelly Blues.* Later, with his regular personnel, Billy cut six more sides for De Luxe, mostly all-vocal, Dexter Gordon and Gene Ammons played a tenor sax chase on *Blowin' The Blues Away;* Dizzy and Johnny Jackson, the alto man, had solos on an instrumental called *Opus X.*

Within its first six months, the Eckstine band became one of the biggest money-making Negro bands in the business; it broke the record at the Earl Theatre in Philadelphia. Billy was a most amiable boss, loyal and unselfish, though the task of handling a band of characters proved to be too much for him at times.

Undeniably it was Billy's singing that was selling the band, along with Sarah Vaughan's; there were regions where bebop registered on the audiences as a strange and meaningless noise, espcially in the southwest, where Charlie Parker recalls, nobody liked it. "In the middle west the colored audiences liked it but the whites didn't," he remembers. "In New York *everyone* liked it." And in the South, of course, Negro audiences still preferred to hear the blues.

After a while on the road, Dizzy began to realize the responsibilities of his position as musical director. He worked hard, sometimes sitting in for a missing pianist or drummer, and trying to make the band sound clean and full. Men like Leo Parker, baritone, Lucky Thompson, tenor, Fats Navarro, trumpet, passed through the line-up. Much of the credit for the band's style was due to the writing of Jerry Valentine and Tadd Dameron.

This, then, was the first big bebop band, though the name of the style was still not in very common use, and there was no mention of the word in my January 1945 review of the band in *Metronome.* Meanwhile small-band bebop was by no means being neglected. Oscar Pettiford was at the Spotlite with Little Benny, Budd Johnson, Clyde Hart and Stan Levey. "All of us were thinking about the new style, trying to get used to playing it," says Oscar. "Clyde was the only pianist that could play those things without any trouble. In fact, he was the first to play the modern style left hand. He told me as long as I was playing that much bass, he didn't need to play rhythm in the left hand and he could just use it to establish the chord changes."

31

Benny Harris did a featured spot with this group in the Spotlite's floor show. The tune was *How High The Moon,* but after four bars of the original melody and an ad lib cadenza, Benny would go into a new theme he'd dreamed up on the *Moon* chords. This theme later became famous under the title *Ornithology,* though Harris has seldom been given the credit he deserves as its composer. Around the same time such bop tunes as *Dee Dee's Dance* and *Little Benny* were coming up, the former written by drummer Denzil Best, the latter a Harris original, the title of which has since been changed to *Ideology.* Both were recorded by Benny on a Savoy session with Oscar, Clyde, Denzil and Budd in October 1944. Benny also wrote the riff based on *Perdido* which has since become a bop standby and was featured as countermelody to the original *Perdido* tune on the Red Rodney-Dave Lambert Keynote recording.

All along 52nd Street, as well as at Minton's and in the Eckstine band, ideas of this kind were springing up. Instead of taking the same old tunes and playing them with the same old opening and closing chorus, these young, keen musicians developed new melodic lines based on the chord sequences of such popular jam numbers as *Stomping at the Savoy, Cherokee* and *All the Things You Are.* The small-band bebop style was definitely established and was rapidly being committed to records, mainly through the activity of Savoy Records, the independent Newark company that had gone on a 52nd Street rampage, cutting every permutation of five or six men that could be assembled.

It had been a gradual thing, perhaps, but it all seemed to have happened very suddenly. In January 1942 and again the following January, Dizzy received exactly one vote in the *Metronome* poll. Ziggy Elman led the field in '43, followed by Roy Eldridge and Cootie. Even the '44 poll gave Diz but six votes. January 1945 found him in tenth place with 68 votes, while Roy, Cootie, Rex and Louis took top honors. Charlie Parker, during all this time, had not received a single vote. But by the beginning of 1945 a movement had started that was to reach proportions unforeseen by bebop's most optimistic well-wishers. It was the year that brought Dizzy enough fans to elevate him to second place in the next poll—second only to Roy Eldridge, his original idol. And in the alto sax voting, Charlie Parker came up from out of nowhere into second place after Benny Carter.

Bebop was taking over Fifty Second Street. Bebop was getting around the country on records, and in the traveling band of Billy Eckstine. But, most important of all, bebop was beginning to win its fight for commercial security. Soon Diz and Bird would not have to work for a salary that was an insult to their great contribution to music. Bebop had begun to climb the last and most significant barrier—the barrier separating it from public acceptance.

32

Chapter IV

"Dizzy," said Billy Shaw, "I think you're about ready to have your own band."

Shaw's timing was perfect. Dizzy, leaving the Eckstine band in the hands of Budd Johnson, had organized his own small group for the Three Deuces, with Charlie Parker, Al Haig, Curly Russell and Stan Levey. He had been signed to a new recording company, Guild, and his first two sides, newly released, were meeting with an enthusiastic reception. They were *Blue 'N' Boogie*, featuring Dexter Gordon and an all-white rhythm section, and *Groovin' High*, Dizzy's bop version of *Whispering*, which featured Bird, Clyde Hart, Remo Palmieri, Slam and Cozy Cole. The last four trumpet measures of *Groovin' High* later provided Tadd Dameron with part of the theme for a beautiful ballad recorded by Sarah Vaughan, *If You Could See Me Now*.

In addition, Diz had been making numerous other dates that were getting his name around among musicians and jazz fans. Having finally found a record company that was willing to give Sarah Vaughan a session (for $20 a side), I had Dizzy on the New Year's Eve date that marked Sarah's debut as a solo singer. Diz also made four sides with Clyde Hart for Manor which later came out under his own name—*Good Bait, I Can't Get Started, Bebop* and *Salt Peanuts*. He even sat in on blues sessions with Rubberlegs Williams and Albinia Jones.

The Deuces engagement was a turning point. The men were only getting $60, with $100 for Dizzy, but by the second week they were raised to $100 with $200 for Diz. The group cut four sides for Guild, with Sid Catlett sitting in on drums and Sarah Vaughan taking the vocal on *Lover Man*. Tadd's *Hot House* (a bop treatment of *What Is This Thing Called Love*,) plus a new *Salt Peanuts* and the fast and dazzling *Shaw Nuff*, made it a memorable session, a perfect example of the new 52nd Street small-band manner, with cleanly played trumpet and alto unison, tricky rhythmic intros and codas, and fantastic solos by Diz, Bird, and Haig. It was The New Jazz in excelsis. Dizzy was on the threshold of success. He even had a personal manager as well as a booker. Milt Shaw, Billy's young son, who had been studying trumpet and trying to learn something from Dizzy, had given up in despair with the comment "I'll never be that good," and decided to work for Diz. The job paid nothing but blood, sweat and tears for quite a while, and it was eight months before Dizzy was able to put Milt on a salary, but their mutual admiration has paid off since then in the form of many successful joint business ventures.

33

The name value of Diz and Bird was given further impetus when the New Jazz Foundation, consisting of disc jockey Symphony Sid, promoter Monte Kay and publicist Mal Braveman, presented two Town Hall concerts in May and June of 1945 starring Gillespie and Parker in performances similar to those on the Guild records. In their enthusiasm for bop and their determination to widen its public, Sid and his colleagues were far ahead of anyone else in the field.

It was while the small group was at the Spotlite, a few doors up the street from the Deuces, that Billy Shaw decided to help Dizzy become a real leader with a full-size orchestra. Bookings came few and far between, however, and Shaw decided to put together a unit, with the Nicholas Brothers, comedians Patterson and Jackson, and June (Mrs. Billy) Eckstine as vocalist. This "package deal" made the Gillespie band acceptable to some of the less cautious bookers. Diz took to the road with a line-up composed of Harry Pryor, Kinny Durham, Elmon Wright and Ed Lewis, trumpets; Al King and Ted Kelly, trombones; Leo Williams and John Walker, altos; Charlie Rouse and Warren Lucky, tenors; Eddie de Verteuil, baritone; Howard Anderson, piano; John Smith, guitar; Max Roach, drums; and Lloyd Buchanan, bass. Walter Fuller wrote all of the arrangements and rehearsed the band. The "Hep-Sations of 1945" took to the road—and headed South.

That meant trouble right from the start. As soon as it was known that the unit would penetrate the Deep South and would have to travel under the most painful Jim. Crow conditions, the men started dropping out like flies. It was hard enough to find trumpet and trombone men who could play fast enough for Dizzy's requirements, but the added problem of finding men who were willing to make the Southern trip made it virtually impossible.

By the time Diz got below the Mason Dixon line he had practically an entire new band. To add to his troubles, promoters told him the customers couldn't dance to this kind of music, so Diz forgot all the fine arrangements in the books and just played the blues.

Dizzy was not yet experienced enough, either, to be successful fronting a big band. Always light-hearted and at ease in earlier jobs, he seemed to tighten up with the responsibility now confronting him. He would take stiff, awkward bows and generally showed no signs of the comic, personable Dizzy of the past.

Later on, in the course of some ninety one-nighters through the southwest with Ella Fitzgerald as co-feature, Dizzy loosened up, started mugging, spinning around and dancing, and became the compleat showman. He even made a big impression at the Apollo, where he had flopped on an earlier appearance. But the problems of personnel and bookings were still too much for both Shaw and

34

Gillespie. As 1945 came to a close he found himself booked with a small band again, on his first trip to California.

Nobody who witnessed Dizzy's stint at Billy Berg's in Hollywood will forget it in a hurry. The booking was an unhappy one from the start. Charlie Parker was in the unit, but was so sick that he showed up either late or not at all on many evenings; as a result, Berg had Dizzy add a tenor, Lucky Thompson, to the group. There were also prejudicial comments made about the presence of two white musicians, Al Haig and Stan Levey, in the group. Ray Brown's bass and Milton Jackson's vibes completed what was musically a very fine combination, but commercially a total flop. On top of all this, Slim Gaillard, who had the alternating group, was not Dizzy's idea of a boon companion. Not long after he and Bird had sat in on a record date with Slim, a tension developed, which was brought to a climax backstage at Berg's when Dizzy characterized Slim as a musical equivalent of Uncle Tom. There was a brief altercation and an even briefer exchange of blows. It seems safe to predict that Dizzy will never again make records with Slim Gaillard.

Bad luck dogged Dizzy again when a new company, Paramount Records, set up an unusual date with Dizzy and a string section to play some Jerome Kern music for a memorial album dedicated to the composer, who had just died. After the records were made, Kern's publishers refused to grant a license for their release, on the grounds that Dizzy had departed from the orthodox Kern melodies.

Dizzy did get to make one successful session on the coast, however, when Ross Russell, who ran a local record shop and had developed an interest in bop, cut several sides with the group for his new Dial label. Made on February 7, 1946, they comprised *Dynamo,* which was a new version of the *Dizzy Atmosphere* cut previously for Guild; *Diggin' For Diz* (a bop *Lover*), *'Round About Midnight, Confirmation,* and *When I Grow Too Old To Dream,* from which title the last word was significantly omitted on the label. Bird didn't make the date, but after the band went back East, he remained on the Coast and cut some sides for Dial a couple of months later.

Business was bad at Berg's. Hardly anybody in California, except a small clique of young musicians, understood or cared about bebop, and the small clique in question earned so little money that it couldn't help Berg's much. Dizzy was not helped by the highly reactionary attitude of local critics and disc jockeys, who were not merely passively disinterested in his work, but actively desirous of seeing him fail. It was a happy day for the Gillespie men when they got back to the Apple.

By now Dizzy's contract with Guild was invalid, the company having gone out of business, and he was due to sign soon with Musicraft. Just in time, I

35

corralled Diz for an album I was recording at Victor, to be called "New Fifty Second Street Jazz." (At that time it would have been useless to try to persuade any major record company to title an album "bebop.") Victor wanted an all-star group featuring some of the Esquire award winners, so we used J. C. Heard on drums and Don Byas on tenor, along with three of Dizzy's own men—Milt Jackson, Ray Brown and Al Haig—and the new guitarist from Cleveland, Bill de Arango. The four sides made on this date were combined with four by a group featuring Coleman Hawkins, Allen Eager, Al McKibbon and others, to make the "New 52nd Street Jazz" package. To the surprise of both RCA Victor and myself, it outsold every jazz album issued in the previous couple of years. Dizzy by now was the object of enough curiosity on the part of musicians who had read or heard about him, to give him a fairly substantial value as a recording artist.

By 1946, bebop recording had reached a phenomenal level both in quantity and quality. Dial on the west coast and Savoy in the east led the field, but Musicraft, Apollo, Black and White, Continental and many of the other companies that had mushroomed since the lifting of the recording ban late in 1943 were going deeper into the market. Norman Granz, the young California impresario, was putting out albums featuring some of the informal performances recorded at his jazz concerts, where the music bordered on bebop. The first album, comprising three twelve-inch sides each of *How High The Moon* and *Lady Be Good* (Stinson Records) became one of the biggest-selling jazz items in years, and was followed by other albums on the Disc, Clef and Mercury labels.

In 1945-46, however, the lines were still not altogether clearly drawn between bebop and the jazz that had preceded it. Musicians like Teddy Wilson, Red Norvo and other swing greats would play dates with Diz and Bird. One Black and White session cut by Joe Marsala even had Dizzy following a piano solo of *Melancholy Baby* by a veteran Dixieland pianist. Later on, the full distinction between the old and new concepts of the rhythm section's function became clear to everyone, as did the difference between the bop and pre-bop conceptions of chord changes and melodic line in improvisation. These facts should be borne in mind when you hear, for instance, a Dizzy record featuring Slam Stewart or some other non-bop musician, in case some tyro to whom you are trying to explain bebop wants to know whether a certain record is bop or not. The answer in such cases, of course, would be "Yes and no," with amplifications.

During this same 1945-46 period, something else happened that helped to take bop out of the small night clubs and small record companies, into the big theatres and ballrooms and onto a major label. For the first time, a great modern jazz orchestra crashed into the juke boxes and even into commercial radio—the band of Woody Herman.

Chapter V

Woody Herman had been around for some eight years as a bandleader before the complete turnabout took place in his style. In the late 30's and early 40's, the Herman herd on Decca records was noted for its ballads, sung by the leader, and its jazz numbers, played in an orchestrated Dixieland form that relied on harmonic and melodic simplicity and a rousing pseudo-New Orleans atmosphere.

Things began to change gradually as Dave Matthews started to write for the band, lifting many ideas from Duke Ellington records. One by one, the old guard dropped out and young, ambitious musicians took their places. After the 1942-43 recording ban, Woody cut a Decca date with Ben Webster sitting in. Chubby Jackson had already joined, and Cliff Leeman was on drums. The style was still not clearly defined; one number could be a Count-inspired *Basie's Basement* while another would be Duke's *I Didn't Know About You,* and a third would suggest the old Lunceford two-beat manner.

Throughout 1944 the evolution continued. Neal Hefti, who had been around Dizzy and Bird, came into the trumpet section and started developing ideas for "head" arrangements. A 21-year-old arranger from Boston, Ralph Burns, took over the piano chair, and gradually the great Herman rhythm section was born, with Billy Bauer on guitar, Dave Tough, and Chubby. The band added to its solo strength with such men as Flip Phillips and Bill Harris. Only one Decca side was cut featuring the revised personnel—*Saturday Night,* made in Hollywood on December 12, 1944—but when Woody switched to Columbia and started cutting in New York two months later, the resulting series of records made jazz history. The five-trumpet unison passage in *Caldonia* marked the first use of outright bebop in a popular best-selling jazz disc. Brilliant instrumental numbers, most of them partly or wholly head arrangements, were waxed under the titles *Apple Honey, Goosey Gander, Northwest Passage.* Ralph Burns contributed such pretty things as *Bijou* for Bill Harris.

There had never been a band like this. It was swinging as no other group ever swung before, and the rhythm section that generated so much of that swing had derived its ideas from the bop school, inserting cross-rhythms and suspensions and doing everything possible to relieve the monotony of the ching-ching-ching-ching rhythm section concept. More important, every man in the band was swinging—and one girl, too, in the person of Marjorie Hyams on vibes.

It is important to remember, however, that this was not strictly a bop band. Harris and Flip were modern, original musicians but few of the characteristics of

37

bop could be found in their work. Of all the soloists, Hefti probably came closest to the bop idiom, and the late Sonny Berman, a great trumpeter whose career was ended so tragically soon, contributed some of the band's most modern and inspired solo moments.

Through '45 and '46 a succession of great men worked with Woody—Pete and Conte Candoli on trumpets; Tony Aless and Don Lamond in place of Burns and Tough; Red Norvo on vibes. Throughout this period, small groups from the band, sometimes with a couple of outsiders added, cut innumerable sessions for Queen, Keynote, Dial, Signature and other labels, under the names of Chubby, Harris or Flip. In 1946 Woody cut some sides of this kind himself, for Columbia, featuring a new young trumpeter-arranger, Shorty Rogers. These sides were released in an album called "Woody Herman & His Woodchoppers."

On March 26, 1946, the Herman band played a Carnegie Hall concert. Igor Stravinsky, impressed by *Caldonia, Bijou* and *Goosey Gander,* was persuaded to write a new work for the herd. The *Ebony Concerto* had nothing to do with jazz, except perhaps in the composer's mind, but it gave the musicians something into which to get their teeth, something to admire and talk about for many months.

Through 1946 the Herman band continued its triumphant establishment of modern big-band jazz as a commercially saleable item. The last recording cut before the group disbanded was, perhaps symbolically, a new Neal Hefti arrangement of *Woodchoppers' Ball,* the blues riff tune for which, because he'd recorded it in Dixieland style in 1939, Woody continued to get requests from older fans. A comparison of the old version on Decca with the new one on Columbia makes a striking illustration of the progress of jazz during those seven years.

While the Herman band was disseminating the new jazz through such unprecedented media as the ABC network, a few other bands were experimenting with the ideas that had been heard around 52nd Street and in the Eckstine orchestra. Boyd Raeburn, former leader of a Mickey Mouse band in Chicago, pulled a surprise by opening at the Lincoln Hotel in New York with a modern group that was willing to experiment in bop. Raeburn even had Dizzy sit in on a record date when he made *Night in Tunisia* and some other sides for Guild. With Little Benny, Oscar Pettiford and Trummy Young in the personnel of Raeburn's mixed group, new ideas abounded. George Handy played piano and arranged, later giving up the piano chair to Ike Carpenter. Several men who were later to find fame in the Herman band were with Raeburn at that time, among them Serge Chaloff, who was experimenting on baritone sax with the ideas he'd heard Bird play on alto; trombonist Ollie Wilson, and a young tenor man named Al Cohen. Later on, the Raeburn band became involved in so much pretentious, impressionistic movie music of the semi-symphonic kind that its bop orientation was forgotten.

38

Contemporary with Raeburn's first and best New York band was the big unit headed by Georgie Auld, a tenor man whose solo and orchestral ideas moved constantly with the times. He, too, took on several outsiders for some Guild sides which, like Raeburn's, were later transferred to Musicraft. *Georgie Porgie* and *In The Middle* boasted a rhythm section composed of Erroll Garner, Mike Bryan, Shadow Wilson and Chubby Jackson and a trumpet team comprising Dizzy, Billy Butterfield, Al Killian and James Roma. Dizzy and Freddy Webster both played on another date when *Co-Pilot* was cut. With men like Tadd Dameron and Vanig Hovsepian (alias Turk van Lake) writing the arrangements, the Auld band was one whose break-up was musically regrettable but economically inevitable. Big band bop, with such rare exceptions as Dizzy and Woody, remained relatively hard to sell even as late as 1948.

On later sessions Auld used Sarah Vaughan for a couple of vocals. The band's final date, cut on June 14, 1946, featured Sarah's *You're Blasé* and an excellent bop original by Neal Hefti, *Mo-Mo*.

It was about the time of Auld's break-up that Charlie Ventura, who had become one of the most popular sidemen in jazz as featured tenor sax star with Gene Krupa, went out on his own with a big band which, though the leader played a compromise style, leaned heavily towards bop in its arrangements. Neal Hefti played in the trumpet section as well as writing such arrangements as *How High The Moon;* this, by the way, was one of the band's National sides, but as was the case with too many bands, its real merit was obscured by poor recording. The excitement along 52nd Street reached fever pitch when, competing with equally strong jazz names at the Deuces, the Onyx and other clubs, the Spotlite Club installed Ventura's 17 men along with another big band, led by Hot Lips Page. Many were the evenings when the musicians outnumbered the customers. Since the club was too small to take more than 75 people, this should go down in jazz history as the most altruistic night club booking ever undertaken. Clarke Monroe, at whose old Uptown House so many bop pioneers had sat in, was the impresario involved.

Later, Ventura gave up the big band in favor of a small group which made a musical and commercial hit through its bop-vocal-with-horns policy.

Incidentally, the same bop idiom that seemed unacceptable to some listeners when dished up in uncompromising orchestral style became popular when it was translated into the modified novelty form of bop vocals. The idea of using the human voice as a wordless jazz instrument goes back to the days of Louis Armstrong's first Okeh records; the swing era produced such notable "scat" singers as Leo Watson; but it was not until January 1945, when Dave Lambert and Buddy

39

Stewart recorded a unison vocal called *What's This?* with Gene Krupa's band, that attention was drawn to the possibilities of singing bop vocally. (Two and a half years later Nat Cole, having discovered bop, answered the Lambert-Stewart question with a similarly-styled opus called *That's What!*)

Bop vocals became popular through the help of the Three Bips and a Bop, a vocal group formed by Babs Gonzales (or Brown), and through the celebrated Ella Fitzgerald treatments of *Flying Home, How High The Moon* and *Lady Be Good* which resulted from her theatre tour with Dizzy. The Gillespie band has found bop singing a commercial asset, and Dizzy has often gone across the boundary from a musical conception into outright vocal comedy. Lambert and Stewart cut some more sides with a small bop band on Keynote, in which the unison singing was effective but the solo vocal not much better than could be produced by any average musician singing in the bathtub. Unfortunately this is true of many bop vocals. With the advent of performances in this idiom by such people as Mel Torme (*That's Where I Came In*) and Johnny Long's band (*Home,* with outright quotes from Babs' *Lop Pow*) the bop vocal had degenerated by 1948 from an amusing novelty into a tiresome and overworked formula. The only exception was the Ventura band, which saved the idea from mediocrity by virtue of Roy Kral's ingenious arrangements for his own voice and Jackie Cain's, blended with the horns.

Although the Ventura, Auld and Raeburn bands were the most heavily loaded with bop material, by 1946 the new jazz had spread so far and wide through records that it was beginning to penetrate some of the popular commercial swing bands. Jerry Mulligan, a saxman and arranger, turned out a boppish *Disc Jockey Jump* for Gene Krupa, whose alto man, Charlie Kennedy, was already the object of some attention from bop students. Even Stan Kenton, whose heavily publicized "Progressive Jazz" has been wrongly defined as bebop by so many non-authorities, would occasionally let his tight, tense band loose long enough to run through a Neal Hefti arrangement of *How High*. (Neal seems determined to go through life making sure that *How High* is in everybody's books.)

Curiously, it was not until some time later that the big Negro bands, aside from Eckstine's and Dizzy's, paid any serious attention to bop. Ellington, Lunceford, Basie and Sy Oliver were too closely identified with a style of their own to make any radical changes; Erskine Hawkins, Buddy Johnson, Lucky Millinder, Andy Kirk, Lionel Hampton, and most of the other favorite bands on the colored theatre circuit, remained faithful to the styles they had established years ago. At the Savoy Ballroom in Harlem, once regarded as a mecca of the best in jazz, the manager glumly reported that his patrons did not go for bop and were more interested in danceable music!

40

Chapter VI

After Dizzy reorganized a big band and made his first records with it in the summer of 1946 (Musicraft) things began to look up. With a stronger personnel and better arrangements, this Gillespie group had a chance to make the grade commercially, especially since Dizzy was developing more and more potentialities as a showman.

Walter Fuller's *Things to Come* showed the real possibilities of modern jazz arranging. Though imperfectly executed at a breakneck tempo, the recording caused a stir among musicians who had previously scorned bop. *Emanon*, on the other side, was a medium-tempo blues showing a somewhat simpler side of big band bop, but swinging all the way. Both numbers showed off individual talents other than Dizzy's, notably that of the vibraharpist Milton Jackson.

Musicraft saw enough possibilities in the Gillespie name to justify the release of an album by Dizzy, featuring both big and small band reissues. Fortified by Billy Shaw's indomitable faith in the band, Dizzy overcame countless obstacles. In Detroit, where the band laid a big egg in July 1946, he returned the following February to produce such a turnout that police had to be called out to keep the crowds from getting out of hand.

With a light-hearted disregard for contracts, Dizzy made records for several small labels in his spare time. On the California Dial date he had been "Gabriel." On Savoy, on a session with Ray Brown, he became Izzy Goldberg. Recording with Tony Scott for Gotham, he was B. Bopstein. On Continental and other labels he simply stuck to John Birks, omitting only his surname. By now fans were in close enough touch with his activities, and familiar enough with his style, to spot these pseudonymous appearances and buy the records promptly.

In January 1947 the ultimate honor came Dizzy's way: he outdistanced Roy to win the *Metronome* poll on trumpet. It was an auspicious opening for an auspicious year. John Lewis, a brilliant young pianist and arranger, joined the band and wrote a *Toccata for Trumpet and Orchestra*. George Russell from Cincinnati penned an Afro-Cuban drums suite, *Cubana Be* and *Cubana Bop*, combining a couple of Dizzy ideas with percussion and chant by Chano Pozo. These works, and others, were premiered when the Gillespie orchestra made its first concert appearance at Carnegie Hall on September 29, 1947, under the auspices of this writer. With Ella Fitzgerald and Charlie Parker also on the bill, a capacity house paid tribute to Dizzy, his arrangers and soloists in an evening of music that proved, as many of us had long suspected, the unrivaled position of his band as an originator in the jazz field.

The band at this time included Howard Johnson and John Brown, altos; James Moody and Joe Gayles, tenors; Cecil Payne, baritone; Dave Burns, Elman Wright, Raymond Orr and Matthew McKay, trumpets; Taswell Baird and William Shepherd, trombones; John Lewis, piano; Al McKibbon, bass, and Joe Harris, drums, plus Milt Jackson on vibes and Kenny "Pancho" Hagood on vocals.

There were still faults, to be sure. The band was rough at times; the overdone bop singing, occasional overarrangement and sometimes tasteless showmanship by the leader were regrettable; but compensating for these shortcomings were some of the most exciting and integrated performances ever created by a big jazz ensemble.

Dizzy and bebop were now a national name, and there was a national movement to get on the bop-wagon. Bop even crept across the fence into the respectable, reactionary world of commercial radio and recordings; Jo Stafford's arrangement of *The Gentleman is a Dope* began with four bars of unmistakably bop riffing. Many other popular singers would find little phrases borrowed from Diz and Bird edging into the backgrounds on their arrangements of a Hit Parade ditty. The Cuban-plus-bop rhythmic alliance, too, was spreading rapidly.

Simultaneously, recording company executives who had scorned bop as uncommercial went on frantic searches for bop talent to sign. Disc jockeys who had held out against the new movement, even including some who had been ardent rooters for Dixieland jazz, suddenly found that bop would pay off, and became ardent Gillespie supporters. One jazz concert promoter, who in previous years had presented nothing but Dixieland bashes and had gone to some pains to insult Dizzy and his supporters at every turn, came to Gillespie's office begging for Dizzy's services at a concert.

Lionel Hampton, in a fantastic interview with a New York paper, was described as "Master of B-bop and Re-bop" and was quoted in such arrant nonsense as this: "B-bop is the chord structure; Re-bop is the rhythm. We combine both and call it the New Movement. Music is nothing but arithmetic—nothing but mathematics." Hampton also made an album of alleged bebop bearing such subtitles as "Zoo-bop," "oo-bop," "re-bop" and "ee-bop," for all of which, according to the program notes, there were "conflicting definitions"!

So fast did the new word catch on with the public, and so frequently was it abused by opportunists, that the result soon was utter confusion. One night on a television show Eddie Condon was introduced as the king of bebop.

National magazines, having heard that Dizzy's followers were aping his whiskers, beret and glasses as well as his trumpet playing, ran feature stories in which the musical importance of bebop was virtually ignored while the eccentricities of some of its followers were exaggerated tenfold. "How Deaf Can You Get?" sneered *Time* in its headline, belatedly acknowledging Dizzy's existence in a piece on bop (May 17, 1948). A nadir in taste, in which Dizzy's own acquiescence must be held partly responsible, was the six-page spread in *Life* magazine in the fall of 1948, which was packed with errors of fact and judgment, culminating in a picture of Dizzy, supposedly a Mohammedan, bowing to Mecca.

Unpleasant though all this cheap publicity might seem, it was no worse than the flood of confusing articles on "swing" that had hit the national presses when that word became a fad a decade or so earlier. At least one can be thankful that the word bebop and the name of Gillespie did get into print often enough to stir up some curiosity about the music, though the average newcomer would have to shed a wealth of prejudices fostered by these articles before perceiving bop's true musical standing.

Bop acquired a permanent New York home in the spring of 1948 through the efforts of Symphony Sid and Monte Kay. At their suggestion, a small bop group was installed at the Royal Roost, a fried-chicken emporium on Broadway which had been experimenting unsuccessfully with non-bop jazz talent. The Tadd Dameron group, featuring Fats Navarro, Allen Eager, Kenny Clarke, Curly Russell and sometimes Charlie Parker, paved the way for a big-name policy at the Roost. Before long the Gillespie, Ventura and Herman bands played the Roost, which became so popular as a bop cynosure that it was soon known as "the house that bop built" and the "Metropolitan Bopera House." In April 1949 the Roost moved its policy across Broadway to the larger Bop City. Bop had taken jazz out of the small 52nd Street clubs and into bigger, better spots where a thousand jazz fans could be entertained nightly.

Bop had spread across the world, too. In England, France, Sweden and a dozen other countries, jazz pundits argued learnedly over the relative merits of the old and the new jazz. Bop was said to be a factor in the violent split between Charles Delaunay, pro-bop head of the French magazine *Hot Jazz*, and Hugues Panassié, the didactic critic and impresario. Rival factions sprang up supporting Delaunay and Panassié, and the feud developed to such a ridiculous point that when Louis Armstrong visited Paris early in 1948 he was given extensive police protection, as a result of a rumor that the new-jazz crowd were out to maim him and prevent him from playing.

In England, bebop produced the customary reaction: most of the musicians

43

were for it and most of the critics against it, with Edgar Jackson, the *Melody Maker* record reviewer, a noteworthy exception in the latter category. That British jazzmen were capable of absorbing the new style was clearly shown in the Jack Parnell Quartet's records such as *Ol' Man Rebop* released here on London, and in some Harry Hayes sides not yet available in this country.

Scandinavia was bop-conscious enough to enable Chubby Jackson to make a successful tour in the winter of 1947-48 with a sextet featuring Frankie Socolow, tenor, Conte Candoli, trumpet, Lou Levy, piano, Terry Gibbs, vibes, and Denzil Best, drums. Just before Chubby left for home, the Gillespie band arrived in Sweden on the first leg of what turned out to be a financially disastrous tour. Many conflicting stories circulated on the band's return, but one fact emerged plainly: the tour was seriously mismanaged, and the reactions to Dizzy's music ranged from outraged indignation to unqualified enthusiasm. Winding up the tour in Paris and the south of France, Dizzy had to cable his booking office for a five-figure sum to get him and the band home. Soon after, he signed with a new manager, Willard Alexander, who had built Benny Goodman and Count Basie in the swing era.

It was during these events in Europe that a new Woody Herman orchestra made its first trip East after being organized in September 1947 on the west coast. Woody, after a year's retirement, had decided to come back with a band that would "gas" everyone, and during 1948 he slowly but surely achieved his objective. Fronting a band full of young, fresh talent, Woody featured himself very little, preferring to allot the solos to such bop experts as Stan Getz, Zoot Simms and Al Cohen on tenors, Serge Chaloff on baritone, Earl Swope on trombone, Shorty Rogers, Ernie Royal and several other talented trumpeters. With Chubby Jackson and Bill Harris in the line-up, and fortified in November by the addition of the amazing Terry Gibbs on vibes and Lou Levy at the piano, the Herman band soon emerged as the cleanest, and perhaps the most effective all around, of the big bands in the bop field. Such records as *Keen and Peachy* and *Four Brothers* gave a slight idea of the band's ability, though they were recorded before the ban, in 1947.

As 1948 came to a close, bebop had achieved recognition and success for which its most ardent sponsors had never hoped. Dizzy had played his first Broadway theatre engagement, drawing big crowds in two successful weeks at the Strand, and following it up on Christmas night with his third Carnegie Hall concert under this reporter's sponsorship. Benny Goodman, quoted a year earlier as strongly anti-bop, formed a new band featuring bop soloists and arrangements. Everywhere, in the United States and Latin America, in Europe and even scattered through Asia, Africa and Australia, young musicians waited for the latest bop

44

orchestrations to arrive, striving eagerly to copy the original Diz and Bird solos, while youthful jazz fans traded rare Savoy and Dial releases for as much as $10 apiece.

Now that bebop has been absorbed into the mainstream of jazz, the major question that remains is how it will expand, escape its limitations and clichés, lead the way into something still richer in musical texture and finer in artistic concept.

If jazz is to remain a separate entity at all, the element of swing, the implied steady beat and tempo, will still be a vital part of every jazz performance, as will the art of improvisation on a given set of chord patterns. Within these confines it may still be possible to develop fertile new ground, as the incorporation of Cuban rhythms has shown. A wider range of instrumentation, with full use of strings and woodwinds, may be one solution; greater variety in thematic bases, and in the tone colors of orchestration, are bound to come. It seems doubtful that jazzmen will be satisfied, a few years from now, to base half their melodies on the chords of *I Got Rhythm, How High The Moon* or the blues.

The story of bop, like that of swing before it, like the stories of jazz and ragtime before that, has been one- of constant struggle against the restrictions imposed on all progressive thought in an art that has been commercialized to the point of prostitution; of struggle against reactionaries who resent anything new which they can neither understand nor perform themselves.

But instead of looking back on these obstacles, it might be better to conclude the story of bebop with a tribute to the wonderful musicians who have overcome them. It is through their uncompromising attitude that you have been given so many hours of invigoratingly new and exciting music. Through their efforts, and their refusal to accept defeat, bebop is here, and it is here to stay.

PART TWO

⫷⫸⫷⫸⫷⫸⫷⫸⫷⫸ ✵ ⫸⫸⫸⫸⫸⫸⫸⫸⫸⫸

how

The first rule to be borne in mind in any discussion of jazz is: Beware of pigeonholes! Any arbitrary attempt to categorize one thing as jazz, another as swing and something else as bebop should be carefully qualified.

That's why it is impossible to answer satisfactorily when someone asks you (as they probably do all too often) the question "What is bebop?" First of all, unless you go into technical details that are incomprehensible to the layman, you can't answer the question at all; secondly, even if you do answer in the form of a technical analysis, you can only say that certain characteristics, when all found in the same piece of music or the same performance, very often constitute bebop. Probably each one of those characteristics can be found in earlier forms of jazz, though you will rarely find them all together except in bebop.

For example, the flatted fifth is nothing new in music, nor is a variation of the customary four-to-the-bar rhythm section pattern. The use of grace notes is not peculiar to bebop; nor is the accenting of upbeats, or the use of passing chords. But if these elements are all intelligently incorporated in a certain manner into a jazz solo, chances are the result will be a bop solo.

Although one of the main advances made by bebop over all preceding jazz is the harmonic development, the fact remains that most bebop improvisation is *based* on a very simple harmonic pattern. It is only the deviations, or implied changes, that give bop its harmonic subtlety.

The outstanding illustration of this is the previously cited fact that about half the bop pieces ever written to date are based on such fundamental chord patterns as *I Got Rhythm* or the blues.

For the less initiated, let's go into the detailed meaning of this statement.

The blues is a basic pattern which has been used in jazz and folk music probably since the late nineteenth century, and certainly during the entire history of ragtime and jazz. The usual form of the blues is a simple theme twelve bars long; of course, it can be played in any key, but as often as not it is played in B Flat, so the following chord pattern is given in that key:

Ex.1

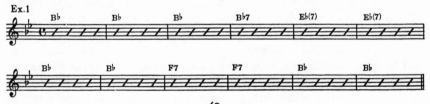

This is the original, basic blues as played in the early days of ragtime—four bars using the tonic chord (adding the seventh in Bar 4), proceeding to the subdominant on the fifth bar, the tonic on the seventh bar and the dominant on the ninth bar, returning to the tonic on the eleventh bar.

As the jazz musician acquired a little more knowledge of music and became tired of this stereotyped pattern, new variations appeared, none of which changed the basic pattern, but all of which helped to make the approach to it a little more oblique. By the late 1930's such musicians as Count Basie, most of whose "original" compositions were based on the blues, used such sequences as the following:

Ex.2

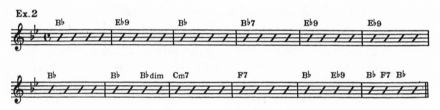

The bebop school has produced an infinity of further variations, of which a typical example follows:

Ex.3

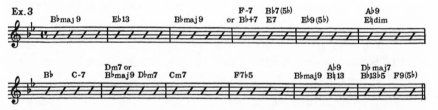

Melodically, the blues has made similar advances. In the days when the blues were first documented by W. C. Handy, the melody was usually built around four notes—the tonic, mediant, subdominant and dominant. The major seventh was never used; the "blue" (flatted) seventh was used incidentally, and by the 1920's it had become fashionable to end on a seventh or ninth chord.

As Handy recalls it in his autobiography, "Father of the Blues" (Macmillan), "The Melody of *Mr. Crump* was mine throughout. On the other hand, the twelve-bar, three-line form of the first and last strains, with its three-chord basic harmonic structure (tonic, subdominant, dominant seventh), was that already used by Negro roustabouts, honky-tonk piano players, wanderers and others of the underprivileged but undaunted class from Missouri to the Gulf, and had become a common medium through which any such individual might express

50

his personal feelings in a sort of musical soliloquy. My part in their history was to introduce this, the 'blues' form, to the general public, as the medium for my own feelings and my own musical ideas."

Mr. Crump later became famous as the *Memphis Blues* in 1912, and was followed by the *St. Louis Blues* in 1914. Later, the blues became more clearly dissociated from its lyrical form and was used extensively as a medium for jazz improvisation, though the vocal form has survived to this day and remains an important factor in American Negro music—such popular singers as Louis Jordan, Dinah Washington and Eddie Vinson used the twelve-bar blues pattern for many of their most popular numbers.

The first blues melodies were constructed, in most cases, to conform with a lyric. Only one of the well known early blues, *Royal Garden Blues,* was so constructed that it lent itself, without any melodic alteration, to the kind of ensemble riffing later practiced by bands in the swing era. However, there are examples on record of such early bands as Fletcher Henderson's around 1924, taking a simple two-bar phrase and orchestrating it, with slight variations in melody so that the notes would. not conflict at any point with the underlying blues chord pattern. For example, a riff like that shown in Ex. 4 would be

Ex. 4   B♭

taken, and fitted to the chord pattern shown in Ex. 1. The first two bars would use Ex. 4 exactly as shown here. The next two bars would be the same, except that the last note would be changed from G to A Flat, to suggest the B Flat seventh chord. In the next two bars the first two notes would be changed from D to D Flat, to suggest the E Flat seventh chord. Bars 7 and 8 could use the original phrase, since they are on the plain B flat chord. Bars 9 and 10 would require an adjustment of the phrase, perhaps along the lines shown in Ex. 5, to

Ex. 5   F7

fit the F Seventh. The final two bars would be the same as the first two, except that the last note would probably be changed from G to B Flat, to suggest finality.

By the swing era, riffs of a more complicated nature were being used, some of them four bars long instead of two, so that they would only fit three times into the regular twelve-bar pattern, instead of having to be repeated six times.

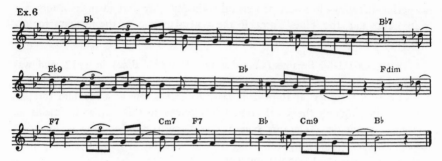

Ex. 6 shows a typical four-bar riff theme of the late 1930's, based on an extension of the melodic idea shown in Ex. 4. Note that the only change made in the four-bar phrase is in the last two notes (bars 4, 8, 12), since this is the only place where a change is essential to conform with the harmonic pattern—i.e., the A and A Flat at the end of bar 4 would sound wrong at the end of bars 8 and 12. The D Flat with which the four-bar phrase opens serves first as a "blue" (flatted) third against the B Flat chord (bar 1), then as a blue seventh in the E Flat Ninth chord (bar 5) and finally as an augmented fifth in the F seventh chord— the rhythm section need not augment this fifth, any more than they need flat the third in bar 1.

Now let's take a bebop melody based on the blues. We find now that the riff, whether two or four bars long, has become almost extinct except as an

THE BEEP

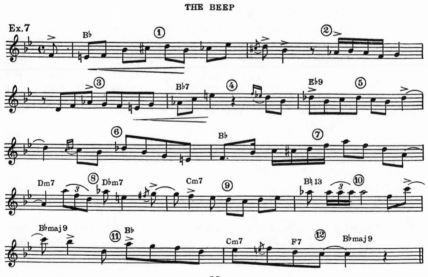

52

occasional background to solos. (One of the few examples of a Dizzy Gillespie composition in the riff idiom is *Dizzy Atmosphere*, which he recorded on Musicraft under that title and also on Dial under the titles *Dynamo A* and *Dynamo B*.) The bebop melody, instead of repeating itself, weaves its way through the twelve-bar format with a continuous melodic line.

Ex. 7, which we'll call "The Beep" for reference, is a typical bop melody based on the twelve-bar blues pattern. Note that the first note of the first bar is the flatted fifth of the B Flat chord and is used as a passing note to the F (fifth). The C Flat and E Flat with which Bar 1 closes are actually the tonic and third of a B Natural chord, suggesting a passing chord half a tone above the key in which the theme is written. It is a common device of bebop to suggest this half tone raise without actually having the rhythm section play it; for instance, a soloist may run an entire G flat arpeggio while the band is in F; but as you see here in bar 2, the resolution into the regular key makes the overall phrase euphonious.

The group of sixteenth notes in bar 2 is actually an outgrowth of the simple phrase shown in bar 1, Ex. 8. In fact, it could just as well be written as in the

Ex. 8

second bar. At a fast or even medium tempo, the difference in effect would be negligible.

The phrase running through bars 3 and 4 is played on and around the notes of the B Flat chord, the A flat being the flatted seventh, G being the sixth and E natural a passing note which ordinarily would lead to an F, but here skips to the sixth, followed by the flatted seventh. Bar 4 ends the phrase on the second beat with a flatted fifth (E natural). In an earlier jazz form this would have led immediately to an F to resolve the phrase, but here the F is left to the imagination —a typical bebop procedure.

Bars 5 and 6 suggest a 3-against-four pattern in the recurrence of an accented D flat three times, each three beats apart. Bars 8 and 9 have the descending sequence of minor sevenths (D minor seventh, D Flat minor seventh and C minor seventh) which has been popularized by bop musicians and has virtually become standard operating procedure at this point in almost every blues chorus played nowadays.

The last four bars start with a typical swinging bop phrase, starting with two anticipated beats (the G and F) and going into a regular sequence of eighth

53

notes for the rest of the ninth bar. Then for sharp contrast the melody shoots up to an A flat in the tenth bar, suggesting either a B Natural 13th or an F Seventh with a flatted third (the rhythm section would probably play the B Natural 13th here).

Notice how the last two bars are filled out, making a complete twelve-bar melody, instead of leaving the last bar or two open or limiting it to one long held note as is often the case with simple riff tunes. The melody ends on a major ninth. Bebop melodies often end on either this chord, a flatted fifth, or a major seventh. Because of the noncomformist nature of bebop and its exponents, you rarely find an ending on the tonic chord; this has become such a fetish that one may well visualize a reaction and find that a few years from now bop musicians will be ending on a flat, unadorned tonic just because it sounds so different!

Needless to say, grace notes can be added to *The Beep* at will, especially on the first note of a series of even eights, or on the first two notes of a phrase such as those at the beginning of Bar 9 or Bar 11.

A careful study of *The Beep* will show why jazz in its present stage can make so much out of so little. The simple twelve-bar blues pattern has provided the basis for a melody which, for complexity, continuity, harmonic and melodic surprises, is immeasurably more interesting than a typical blues of ten or twenty years ago, so much so that the entire character of the music has been changed, it has acquired a different name, *bebop,* and those who cannot follow such departures from the norm claim that it is no longer jazz. Musicians who deplore the limitations of jazz, claiming that its confinement in such formats as the blues has prevented it from developing as an art form, should be heartened by a comparison of a bebop blues with a riff blues or a ragtime blues. They may even end up convinced that the blues is no confinement at all.

Next to the blues, the most widely used chord formation for a bebop piece is undoubtedly that of *I Got Ryhthm*. In fact, it is hardly fair to refer to it by this title, since George Gershwin did not invent the tonic chord,and the chord sequence in question is virtually built around this single chord for 24 of its 32 bars, thus:

Ex.9

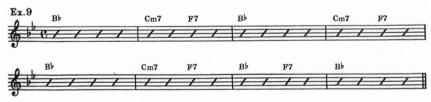

This eight-bar phrase is repeated twice, then comes the release (also known as the bridge, or channel, or middle eight), and then comes a repeat of the first eight bars. The commonest release, used in the original *I Got Rhythm,* consists of two bars each of D Seventh, G Seventh, C Seventh and F Seventh. Often the first two chords are B Flat Seventh and E Flat, followed by the C Seventh and F Seventh.

This pattern, known among modern musicians simply as "rhythm," is indigenous to all jazz and still obtains, with variations and complications, as a basis for innumerable bebop works, many of them so intricate melodically that it's hard to believe they started out as variations of *I Got Rhythm.* Indeed, it would be fairer to say that they didn't start out that way, since no musician has the *melody* of *I Got Rhythm* in mind when he constructs his own theme or improvisation. He merely has in mind the chord pattern (Ex. 9), beyond which everything is his own invention.

This formula has been used for such well known bop tunes as *Shaw Nuff, Anthropology, 52nd Street Theme.*

Many bop musicians, tiring of the endless sequence of three simple chords as shown in Ex. 9, have inserted harmonic variations such as Ex. 10. As the treble clef shows, this chord pattern gives the musician scope for some melodic ideas far more interesting than he could build on the simpler chords of Ex. 9.

The particular chord pattern shown in Ex. 10 has been used to good effect on records featuring Don Byas, Fats Navarro and others.

In recent years it has been an increasingly common practice to take some definite chord sequence of a well-known song (usually a standard old favorite) and build a new melody around it. Since there is no copyright on a chord sequence, the musician is entitled to use this method to create an original composition and copyright it in his own name, regardless of who wrote the first composition that used the same chord pattern. Following is a table of some of the outstanding examples, in recent jazz years, of this practice as reflected in well known recordings.

Title	Recorded by	On	Is Based on Same Chords As
Little Willie Leaps	Miles Davis	Savoy	All God's Children Got Rhythm
Suburban Eyes	Thelonious Monk	Blue Note	All God's Children Got Rhythm
Charge Acount	Dave Lambert & Buddy Stewart	Keynote	All the Things You Are
Blue Serge	Mad Monks	Dial	Cherokee
Dial-Ogue	Ralph Burns	Dial	Cherokee
Ko-Ko	Charlie Parker	Savoy	Cherokee
Keen and Peachy	Woody Herman	Columbia	Fine and Dandy
Lester Blows Again	Lester Young	Aladdin	Honeysuckle Rose
Bean At the Met	Coleman Hawkins	Keynote	How High the Moon
Bird Lore	Charlie Parker	Dial	How High the Moon
Hopscotch	Vivien Garry	Sarco	How High the Moon
Indiana Winter	Esquire All Stars	Victor	How High the Moon
Low Ceiling	Beryl Booker	Victor	How High the Moon
Ornithology	Charlie Parker	Dial	How High the Moon
Slightly Dizzy	Joe Marsala	Musicraft	How High the Moon
Bean Stalking	Coleman Hawkins	Asch	Idaho
Booby Hatch	Allen Eager	Savoy	Idaho
Rampage	Allen Eager	Savoy	I Found A New Baby
Five Zillion numbers	Everyone	All labels	I Got Rhythm
Donna Lee	Charlie Parker	Savoy	Indiana
Ice Freezes Red	Fats Navarro	Savoy	Indiana
Trumpet at Tempo	Howard McGhee	Dial	Indiana
Tiny's Con	Aaron Sachs	Manor	Indiana
Evidence	Thelonious Monk	Blue Note	Just You, Just Me
Spotlite	Coleman Hawkins	Victor	Just You, Just Me
Mad Be-Bop	J. J. Johnson	Savoy	Just You, Just Me
Ray's Groove	Babs Gonzales	Apollo	Just You, Just Me
Overtime	Met. All Stars	Victor	Love Me or Leave Me
Diggin' For Diz	Tempo Jazz Men	Dial	Lover
Bean and the Boys	Coleman Hawkins	Sonora	Lover Come Back to Me
Bird Gets the Worm	Charlie Parker	Savoy	Lover Come Back to Me
Flight of the Be-Bop	Billy Taylor	HRS	Lullaby in Rhythm
Sportsman's Hop	Coleman Hawkins	Asch	Lullaby in Rhythm
A Bebop Carroll	Tadd Dameron	Savoy	Mean To Me
Ol' Man Rebop	Dizzy Gillespie	Victor	Old Man River
Victory Ball	Met. All Stars	Victor	'S Wonderful
Stupendous	Charlie Parker	Dial	'S Wonderful
Jack Pot	Charlie Ventura	Savoy	Stomping at the Savoy
Byas a Drink	Don Byas	Savoy	Stomping at the Savoy
Sweet & Hot Mop	Stan Hasselgard	Capitol	Sweet and Lovely
Step On It	Coleman Hawkins	Manor	Tiger Rag
Hot House	Dizzy Gillespie	Musicraft	What Is This Thing Called Love
Groovin' High	Dizzy Gillespie	Musicraft	Whispering
Stompy	Coleman Hawkins	Signature	Whispering

THE BOP BEAT

The most difficult step in the transition from the old to the new jazz is the acquisition of a feeling for the bop beat. Melodically, an old-time jazzman may be able to memorize a few bop clichés and lend a superficial bop touch to his solos, but rhythmically, he finds it almost impossible to change what may have been a lifelong instinct for a certain rhythmic feeling in his improvisations.

A main characteristic of bepop rhythmically, as we have pointed out, is the change from "hot jazz" to "cool jazz," effected in a lag-along style that may tend at times to get slightly behind the rhythm section's beat. Many perfect examples can be found in the recordings of Erroll Garner, the great pianist who, strangely enough, is not a bop man from the melodic standpoint. There are some passages in which Garner's right hand may delay the melody line by almost a full eighth note, so that, for example, a passage that he conceives (and the listener feels)

Ex. 11

as Ex. 11 will be played so that, technically, it would be closer to the truth to write it as in Ex. 12.

Ex. 12

Another important rhythmic effect much used by bop soloists is the up-beat accent. (When a measure consists of eight notes, "one-and-two-and-three-and-four-and," the up-beats are the "ands"). These up-beats are accented slightly more than the down-beats, and are phrased as shown in Ex. 13, which is Frank

Ex. 13
Medium tempo

Paparelli's transcription of the introduction to Dizzy's record *Oop Bop Sh'Bam.* The triplet phrasing of the eight notes in Bar 2, with accents on the up-beats, may often be found written as dotted eighths and quarters (Gil Fuller uses this notation in transcribing the same passage for the orchestration of *Oop Bop Sh'Bam*) and are sometimes written as straight eighth notes; but, no matter how you see them on paper, Ex. 22 shows how they are generally expected to sound.

This up-beat effect occurs more often in medium and medium-fast tempos. At faster tempos you often find groups of eighth notes evenly phrased and accented, except that in each group of four eighth notes, the second note is unaccented or "ghosted" so that it is hardly heard at all. This is sometimes indicated in the notation by the use of parentheses around the note, as shown in Ex. 14. On

Ex.14

occasion, a larger proportion of notes may be ghosted, even two or three consecutively; the ghost walks intriguingly through some of Pete Candoli's work on *Dee Dee's Dance* and *Boomsie* (Rainbow).

Double-time, originally used only in slow tempos but now featured in almost any tempo by the more skilled bebop technicians, is a manner of playing a solo as if the chorus contained twice as many bars, each two beats long; in other words, as if the rhythm section were placing twice as many accents as it actually does.

Ex. 15

Ex. 15 shows the release of Dizzy's trumpet solo on *One Bass Hit*, the first four bars of which are in double-time. Paparelli has given Dizzy the benefit of the doubt on several notes which are actually either "ghosted" or not played at all, or, leave us face it, fluffed. When you are playing at a speed of twelve notes per second, as Dizzy does here, it is not unlikely that an occasional error or omission will occur in a long sequence of sixteenth notes, and that it will pass too fast for the average human ear to perceive it, provided the great majority of notes can be heard and identified as correctly played and phrased.

Notice how, after the four-bar spell of double-time, Dizzy reverts to the normal beat, playing mostly eighth notes, for the rest of the release. Double-time is used for contrast, and like so many other devices in every kind of music, is only effective when the artists knows how and when to employ it discreetly.

Underneath all the above-mentioned facets of the bop beat lies the all-important bop beat of the rhythm section, differing vastly from the dry, monotonous 4-4 of earlier rhythm sections. In the old days the drummer frequently played high hat cymbal for the second and fourth beat accents, and underlined the whole rhythm section with a bass drum beat on the first and third, or on all four beats; today the top cymbal is used in place of the bass drum to establish the beat, and in a much more legato manner, one beat merging into another as the cymbal vibrates throughout an entire chorus.

The bass drum, high hat cymbals, snare drum and all the other equipment at the drummer's disposal are used for the wide variety of rhythmic and tonal accents that punctuate the typical bop chorus and provide the soloist with the excitement and stimulus conducive to a great performance.

This change in the style of drumming is the most important new feature of the jazz rhythm section. The changed function of the pianist from a steady swing left hand to special punctuations has already been discussed. The guitar, used less frequently nowadays as a rhythm instrument, is employed like the piano to "feed" or "bop" the soloists by "comping" with irregularly accented chords. The bass fulfills the same function as in earlier rhythm sections, generally supplying a steady, clear-toned four beats to the bar (except, of course, when it steps out for solo passages or special fills).

For examples of the modern function of the rhythm section, most of the small band records on Savoy and Dial are worth studying, especially Charlie Parker's *Relaxing at Camarillo* date on Dial. This includes Barney Kessel's guitar, in one of the regrettably rare examples of intelligent use of this instrument in a bop rhythm section. For big band rhythm sections, listen to any recent Woody Herman release, and to some of Dizzy's Victor and Musicraft sides—at least those that don't feature Cuban percussion effects, which, though often a welcome musical effect, are not relevant to the subject of bebop.

BOP PHRASING AND CONSTRUCTION

One of the most vital qualities of bop improvisation and composition is its variety of construction. (Since most single-line bop compositions were originally improvisations that somebody took the trouble to memorize or write down, there is no difference in the character of a bop melody line whether it's a set theme or an ad lib chorus.)

An outstanding example of bop construction is *Anthropology*, by Dizzy and Bird. Although based on a thirty-two bar pattern similar to *I Got Rhythm*, it departs · in almost every respect from the previous orthodox rules for a jazz composition. Ex. 16 shows the melody together with a piano accompaniment transcribed by Frank Paparelli, from J. J. Robbins' trumpet solo edition.

ANTHROPOLOGY

Ex. 16

Transcribed by
Frank Paparelli

DIZZY GILLESPIE
CHARLIE PARKER

61

The thirty-two bars are divided into the A-A-B-A pattern, i.e. an eight-bar passage followed by a repeat (save for a variation in the last two bars), then an eight-bar release, and finally a repeat, with slight concluding variation, of the original eight bars.

If you listen to the Gillespie recording (in Victor's New 52nd Street Jazz album) while following the music, you will see how the rhythm section emphasizes certain aspects of the melody, such as the tricky, unexpected rhythmic phrase in Bar 2, in which the bass drum underscores the two F's of the melody.

The eight-bar passage which establishes the main melodic theme consists roughly of five phrases. The first starts right on the first beat of bar 1. The second is the short three-note phrase in bar 2, starting on an anticipated third beat of the measure. Then comes another two-bar phrase, starting on the second eighth note of the measure. The next phrase starts with an anticipation of the first beat in bar 5, and the last phrase starts with a three-beat pickup into an on-the-beat quarter note on the first beat of bar 7. Thus every phrase lends variety to the melody by starting at a different part of the measure. Needless to say, this was not a calculated effect, but the composer (or composers; I don't know who wrote which part of the tune) instinctively felt that this would sound right. Compare this construction with a swing composition such as *Stomping at the Savoy*, which consists of the same simple two-bar phrase repeated with slight melodic variations, and with no change of accent, until the eight bars are filled.

In the fourth measure, the four eighth notes (D, A, C and B) seem to constitute an uncompleted phrase, on paper; actually, however, they are a syncopation of Ex. 17 (A), and in the past it has been customary to write this syncopation

Ex. 17   A   B

as in Ex. 17 (B), tying the last note over onto the third beat of the bar. However, since bop musicians usually cut these anticipated notes short, it is more correct technically, though perhaps a little more confusing visually, to write it as four eighth notes followed by a whole beat rest.

After you have studied this eight-bar establishment of the melody, examine the underlying chords played by the piano. To illustrate the fact that many different chord patterns can be used for variety, I have also appended (Ex. 18) the piano part of Gil Fuller's orchestration on the same tune. In both the Paparelli and Fuller piano parts you will notice the lack of any steady four-beats-to-the-bar

(CONTINUED ON NEXT PAGE)

64

rhythm; the piano "comps" or punctuates rhythmically, with frequent anticipations of the beat, relieved by on-the-beat chords which maintain a pleasing balance between syncopation and steady rhythm.

Notice, too, that harmonically the bop rhythm section likes to move in straight lines; for instance, at Letter "A" in Fuller's piano part, instead of the conventional B Flat, G Minor Seventh, C Minor Seventh and F Seventh which would normally be the way to lead back into the B Flat chord (Ex. 19 shows the bass progression

Ex. 19

on these chords), you find the first B Flat chord followed by a D Flat Ninth, C Minor Seventh and B Seventh, so that the bass part moves chromatically from D

Ex. 20

down to B Flat (Ex. 20). And then, instead of a B Flat chord, you again find the major seventh added. Boppers abhor a straight tonic as passionately as nature abhors a vacuum.

The second eight bars is a repeat of the first eight, except that the last two bars of the phrase are changed; here again the melodic approach is unconventional, for instead of ending on the tonic, as usually happens at the end of the second eight bars, the passage ends with a D in the key of C, implying a C Major Ninth.

Now examine the melody of the release, starting with the anticipated G Sharp (F Sharp concert) which immediately establishes the D Seventh. (Rhythm section adds flatted fifths to all the main chords of the release, which are D Seventh, G Seventh, C Seventh and F Seventh). Here we find first a two-bar phrase starting with this syncopation, and ending with a "bebop" (two eighth notes on the first beat of the bar) and then for contrast, we have a phrase that starts with a pickup eighth note but no syncopation, but ends with a syncopation, anticipating the first beat of Bar 20. Then suddenly the melody leaps up unexpectedly to an A concert played three times and anticipated each time; this creates a rhythmic suspension that leads excitingly into the second half of the release. Bar 22 is a slight variation, rhythmically, of bar 21; following these two one-bar phrases we find a longer phrase, moving downward melodically from E Flat concert to A, the first note anticipated and accented by both the horn(s) and the accompanying rhythm.

After studying this entire chorus carefully, examine next Dizzy's ad lib solo on the same record, reproduced in Ex. 21. This starts out with two very simple

65

Ex. 21

phrases which have no bop characteristics; the first in fact, is a quote from *The Gold Digger's Song* (*We're In The Money*), and the next in bars 3-4, is a variation. Dizzy spends these four bars, in effect, just warming up, preparing himself and his listeners for the fireworks that are to follow. To increase the suspense he waits a whole measure, leaving bar 5 tacet and then plunging into a downward cascade of sixteen eighth notes, ending on a tonic which anticipates the first beat of bar 8. The second eight bars, like the first, start with a short, simple phrase (bar 9), but by now Diz is wound up; he launches a phenomenal phrase which not only finishes out the eight bars but continues without interruption halfway through the release. Bars 10 to 19 are thus linked together, although at the sixteenth bar Dizzy indicates the impending release by playing a note from the D Ninth chord, two beats ahead of its actual place in the chord pattern of the tune, and holding it over into the seventeenth bar, at which point the rhythm section plays a D Seventh or Ninth.

After a five-and-a-half-beat rest, Diz plays the second half of the release as a three-bar phrase, taking another comparatively long breathing spell (five and a half beats again) before jumping up an octave for a startling series of triplets on bars 25, 26 and 27; this develops into a long phrase of eighth notes and occasional triplets which overlaps into the first beat of bar 1 of the following chorus.

INTERVALS

One of the greatest charms of many bebop compositions is the use of unusual intervals in the melodic line. Reduced to the simplest possible terms, this means that the next note in the melody turns out to be much higher, or much lower, than you expected. Instead of moving in predictable contours, with a steady flow of ups and downs, a bop melody may make sudden and refreshing jumps of a sixth, seventh, octave or more, up or down—in other words, the space or interval between two notes of the melody may have a lot to do with its originality.

A fine example is *That's Earl, Brother* (Ex. 22). The melody begins with an emphasis on the interval of a fourth—B to F Sharp, C to G, D Flat to A Flat and D to A, each of these pairs of notes linked by an unaccented series of lower notes (the D, E, F Natural and F Sharp respectively). The melody then rises to the tonic and descends through bar 4. Bars 5 and 6 have a melodic range of only a major seventh, but in bars 7 and 8 there is an entirely unexpected jump upwards and a delightfully circuitous return to the lower register. In fact, the intervals in bars 7 and 8 are the high spot of the entire composition.

In the release there is another beautiful sweeping phrase at bar 19, starting on the low A and then rising in thirds and fourths up to the G, and just as unexpectedly down to the B. For the second half of the release, in complete contrast

67

Ex. 22

with the first half, the melody runs up three minor ninth chords, then changes its pattern again in bar 24 to link with the pickup notes of the final eight-bar phrase.

PASSING NOTES

One of the fundamental advances of bebop over earlier jazz lies in its use of passing notes and passing chords. A passing note is one which does not belong in the chord, but which is used to pass up or down onto one of the notes of that chord. (If it passes up or down through an interval of more than a major second, it is known as an *added* note.)

For simplicity, let's take the chord of C Major, consisting of the notes C, E and G. To these you can add the sixth (A), the major seventh (B), the ninth (D), any or all of which are frequently added by the rhythm section as well as being used in the solo line. Ex. 23 shows how every note in the chromatic scale can be

Ex.23

Melody

Sust.
Background

used against what was originally a simple C chord. The melody line uses F, D Sharp, D Flat, B Natural, B Flat, A Flat and F Sharp as passing notes, while the accompanying harmony adds an A, a B and a D to the original C-E-G triad. In other words, if you know how to place them and in what order to use them, there is no such thing as a "wrong note" or a "note off the chord"!

Also, the soloist can play notes implying chords that are not actually played by the rhythm section. For example, in Ex. 24, on the last two beats of Bar 1 the

Ex.24

soloist plays a D Flat chord against the rhythm's C chord, and at the end of the second bar he plays a B chord, also against the C. At a fast bop tempo, these added chords are so quickly resolved that you don't have time to hear any harmonic conflict. On the other hand, if Ex. 24 were played at a slow tempo, with the rhythm section reiterating the C chord distinctly on all four beats of each bar, the effect would be disastrous.

It is because passing notes are used by bop musicians *without* resolving to the notes to which they are supposed to "pass" that people think they hear wrong notes in bebop. In Ex. 25, the first bar shows how, following the D Flat, which is

Ex.25

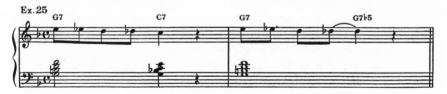

"off the chord" of G Seventh, you would naturally expect to pass to another note which is either in the G Seventh chord, or else in another chord that follows logically after a G Seventh—in this case, a C in the chord of C Seventh. But in the second bar you see how a bopper stays on the D Flat, which thus becomes a "dissonant" note—in the chord of G Seventh it is the flatted fifth.

The more you listen to bebop, the more you will be impressed with the change that has been effected in the whole character and sound of jazz improvisation by the acceptance of this flatted fifth as a "right" note instead of a wrong one. When you reflect what a large proportion of chords in any jazz number are sevenths, (or ninths) and how many variations can be produced by the inclusion of the flatted fifth in your ad libbing on each of these chords, you may will understand why the flatted fifth has become practically synonymous with bebop.

Obviously the flatted fifth is nothing new in music as a whole, but it is relatively new in jazz. When Oscar Moore, striking a final chord on the original King Cole version of *Sweet Lorraine* in 1940 (Decca), played a ninth with a flatted fifth, it seemed to many listeners like a delightfully novel way to end a performance. Today, flatted-fifths as a concluding chord are the rule rather than the exception.

Another very important change in jazz improvisation is the use of minor sevenths as passing chords; for example, study Ex. 26. If you look at the top line

horizontally—that is, without regard to the bass line—the groups of sixteenth notes will appear to be based on a B Minor Seventh, E Minor Seventh, A Minor Seventh and D Minor Ninth respectively. But if you read these notes vertically—that is, looking at each treble note separately with regard only to what's below it in the bass clef, and without regard to what follows it—you'll see that, for instance, the A is simply an eleventh on top of the E Seventh chord; the F Sharp is a ninth, the D a seventh and the B a fifth. In other words, this whole business of relative minor sevenths simply amounts to the use of elevenths; similarly, in the fourth bar, the notes E-C-A-F in the treble, which appear to indicate a D Minor ninth, actually represent a G seventh with the thirteenth, eleventh and ninth added.

The diminished chord, for no apparent reason, is used less frequently in bebop than in earlier jzzz. Augmented chords are used, however, and as Ex. 27

shows, if you add a flatted fifth to an augmented ninth chord you have a double-augmented, and as the example shows (shifting the D down an octave to make the picture clearer) this is, in effect, a whole tone scale, i.e., a sequence of notes a whole tone apart.

This double augmented, or whole tone scale, has been used for some weird effects in bebop. A simpler example occurs in the final chorus of *One Bass Hit*, in the last two bars of the release (Ex. 28), when a three-against-four rhythmic

pattern is built with groups of three notes building upwards on a G double augmented (i.e., the whole tone scale of G, A, B, C Sharp, D Sharp and F).

More complex examples of melodies on the double augmented can be heard in the release of the first chorus on Dizzy's *52nd Street Theme* (Victor), and the release of the last chorus on Clyde Hart's *Dee Dee's Dance* (Savoy).

On the same record of *52nd Street Theme*, by the way, you will hear one of bop's few examples of polytonality. While Dizzy plays the two-bar riff theme in the key of C, Milton Jackson plays the same melody on vibes in the key of G Flat—i.e., a flatted fifth away from the rest of the band. This has the effect of making the whole thing sound as though it is built on a double-augmented. Polytonality is as yet rare in jazz; however, polyphony has found its way into bop occasionally, as in *Chasing The Bird* (Savoy) which has Charlie Parker and Miles Davis playing two different melodies simultaneously. Needless to say, polyphony was a main feature of Dixieland jazz, in which three or four horns would improvise at once, but it was disorganized polyphony with inconsistent results.

A careful study of the melodic, harmonic and rhythmic characteristics we have cited, and of the records mentioned in this chapter, should give you a fairly comprehensive grounding in the overall musical texture of bebop. For fuller details (Walter Fuller details, that is) you can delve into the subject more deeply, and find out how to combine your bebop knowledge with the art of big-band

71

orchestration, by studying Walter "Gil" Fuller's bebop arranging method, a companion to this volume, issued by the same publisher.

In case any of the foregoing pages have given you the impression that complexity of construction or phrasing is essential to a bop performance, don't forget that four entire bars of *Oop Bop Sh'Bam*—in fact, half the main theme—consists simply of three notes, the triad of A, C and E. By varying the lengths of these notes, their placing and accents, it was possible to build a very pleasing theme. (Ex. 29). Similarly the themes of Dizzy's *Salt Peanuts* and *Dizzy Atmosphere*,

Ex.29

Charlie Parker's *The Hymn,* are about as generous as Jack Benny in their use of notes. Complexity in itself is no virtue, any more than technical prowess, but find the right contrast between complexity and simplicity, plus the right way to use your technical knowledge, and you're in!

One concluding thought: don't ever be scared, in playing bop, that you are breaking the rules, or that a certain passage is not strictly bop. Be a pragmatist. Remember that as far as Diz and Bird were concerned, rules were only made to be broken; moreover, some of their most successful effects have been achieved by the contrasting insertion of non-bop passages such as the intro and coda on *Shaw Nuff,* the comedy vocals on *Salt Peanuts* and *When I Grow Too Old To,* and the special rhythms in *Night In Tunisia, Manteca* and many others. Remember that if in the middle of a great bop chorus you suddenly hear four bars of *Moon Over Miami* or *Shine on Harvest Moon,* it's because the soloist just happened to think of it and figured that it fitted into the scheme of the chorus. (Or maybe he'd just run out of ideas. Nobody's infallible).

Remember, in short, that nobody ever gave Diz or Bird a lesson in the art of blowing a jazz chorus. They learned by listening to the jazzmen who preceded them, then they added ideas of their own. You can, in turn, build on the wonderful foundation that the Gillespies and Parkers have provided. From there on out, it's up to you.

PART THREE

⋘⋘⋘⋘⋘⋘⋘ ✿ ⋙⋙⋙⋙⋙⋙⋙

Who

Teddy Hill's band at the Apollo Theatre in New York City, 1940. Trumpets are AL KILLIAN, JOE GUY and DIZZY. Drummer is KENNY "KLOOK" CLARKE.

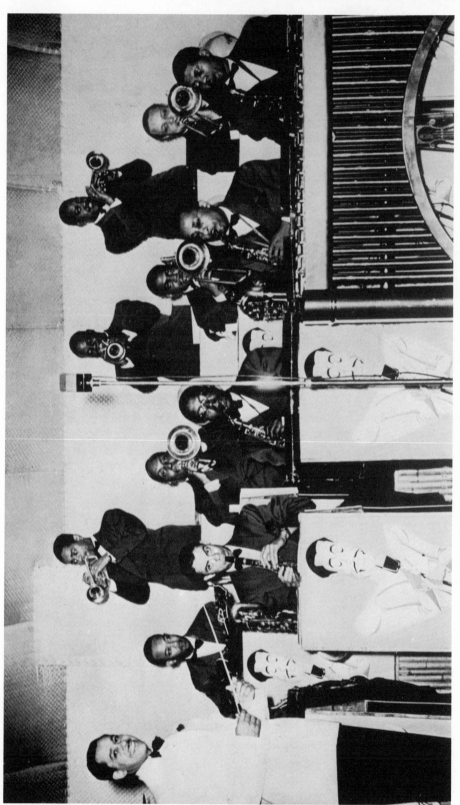

Dizzy with Cab Calloway's orchestra, 1941. Clarinetist is JERRY BLAKE; guitar, DANNY BARKER; TYREE GLENN is middle trombonist.

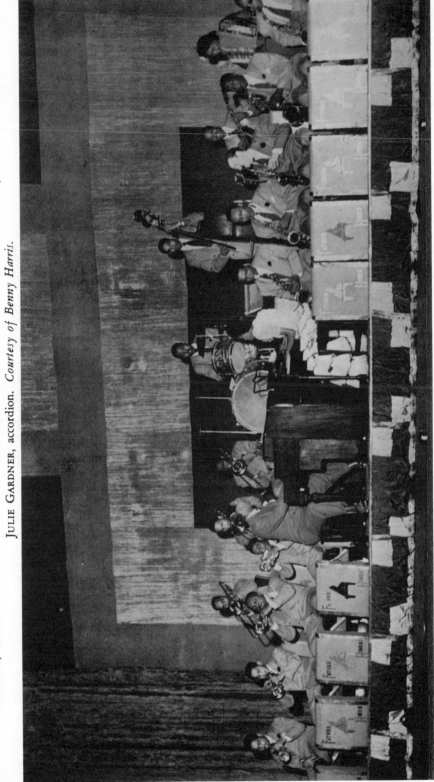

Earl Hines' opening at the Apollo, April 23, 1943. Trumpets are DIZZY, BENNY HARRIS, GAIL BROCKMAN, SHORTS MC-CONNELL. Pianos, EARL HINES and SARAH VAUGHAN. Saxes: A. CRUMP, ANDREW GARDNER, SCOOPS CAREY, JOHN WILLIAMS, CHARLIE PARKER. Trombone next to drummer SHADOW WILSON is BENNY GREEN. JESSE SIMPKINS, bass; JULIE GARDNER, accordion. *Courtesy of Benny Harris.*

The Earl Hines band of 1943 with DIZZY, BENNY HARRIS, GAIL BROCKMAN and SHORTS MCCONNELL on trumpets, GUS CHAPPELL and BENNY GREEN on

1945." Left to right: LLOYD BUCHANAN, bass; MAX ROACH, drums; JOHN SMITH, **gutar**. AL KING and TED KELLY, trombones. EDDIE DE VERTEUIL, CHARLIE ROUSE, LEO WILLIAMS, JOHN WALKER, WARREN LUCKY, saxes. HARRY PROY, KINNY DURHAM, DIZZY, ELMAN WRIGHT and ED LEWIS, trumpets. HOWARD ANDERSON, piano; WALTER FULLER, arranger. *From Les Zimmerman, William Morris Agency, Inc.*

Georgie Auld's band at the Three Deuces, 1946, with CURLY RUSSELL, GEORGE WALLINGTON, SERGE CHALOFF, TINY KAHN and RED RODNEY. *Courtesy*

There could be· no such thing as a complete biographical index of bebop musicians. New, youthful bop stars are appearing so frequently that it is impossible to keep pace with developments. It is also very hard to draw a line between bop musicians and others; for instance there are men like Ben Webster and Coleman Hawkins whose influence on modern jazzmen seemed substantial enough to justify their inclusion.

On the other hand, there are important men like Willie Smith, Woody Herman and Buck Clayton who, though they have been closely associated with bop musicians, do not play in this style themselves and have not influenced the musicians who do. Most of these stars' biographies being familiar through frequent retelling in magazines and books, the information has been excluded here to make room for less widely publicized data.

The only claim for this department, then, is that it covers virtually every instrumental star in bebop who has acquired a reputation in this field through a substantial number of recordings. Inevitably, because most records are made in New York or Los Angeles, many talented artists elsewhere may have been omitted.

Records originally released on	May also be found on
Guild	Musicraft
Regis	Manor
Bel-Tone	Majestic
Majestic	Mercury
Clef	Mercury
Keynote	Mercury
Asch	Stinson
Manor (Dizzy date)	Columbia
Vocalion	Okeh
Continental	Lenox

ABBREVIATIONS

b.	born
rec.	records, recorded
w.	with
comp.	composed
faves.	favorite musicians
JATP	Jazz at the Philharmonic concert album.
WNEW	Saturday Night Swing Session Album recorded from WNEW broadcasts, 1947.

Note: Charles Delaunay's *New Hot Discography* (Criterion, $6) is an indispensable guide to practically all recorded jazz through 1947, and the recording ban was in effect throughout 1948. Therefore, no attempt is made below to chronicle every record made by the artists listed. In as many cases as possible, the record titles listed are those which, *in the artist's own opinion,* offer the best recorded examples of his work.

EUGENE AMMONS, tenor sax; b. Chicago, 1926. Son of Albert Ammons, boogie-woogie pianist who has appeared at Carnegie Hall, Cafe Society, etc. Gene was with King Kolax, 1943, but first came to prominence in the Eckstine band, playing chase choruses with Dexter Gordon on *Blowin' the Blues Away* (De Luxe). Led own small groups around Chicago, 1947-48, also played at Three Deuces, NYC. Rec. *El Sino, Wild Leo, Leaping Leo* with Leo Parker (Savoy); *Concentration, Blowing Red's Bop,* own group (Aladdin); *Red Top, Idaho* and numerous other sides by own group (Mercury); also a session with his father on Mercury.

IRVING ASHBY, guitar; b. Somerville, Mass, Dec. 29, 1920. New England Conservatory. Lionel Hampton, 1940-42; featured on Hamp's Sextet sides (Victor). Mostly free-lancing around LA until joined King Cole, 1947. Featured in blues JATP Vol. VI (Clef); also made Junior Jazz album (Black & White 12-inch); Andre Previn album (Sunset), and dates w. Fats Waller (Victor 12-inch) and Lester Young (Aladdin). In addition to musical talents, is a qualified meteorologist.

GEORGIE AULD, tenor & alto sax; b. Toronto, May 19, 1919. Settled in Brooklyn, 1929. Won Rudy Wiedoft scholarship on alto, 1931. Tenor, 1935, after hearing a Hawkins record. Own band at Nick's; w. Bunny Berigan, 1937-8; many Victor records. Artie Shaw, 1938-9. Took over Shaw band, 1940, then led new group of his own. W. Jan Savitt briefly, then Benny Goodman, mid-1940, for a year, making great sextet sides w. Charlie Christian, Cootie Williams, Count Basie (Columbia). Rejoined Shaw, 1941-2; Army, 1943. Own big band, 1944-6; semi-inactive since then, working briefly at Three Deuces early 1948. Style on tenor has changed progressively and by 1948 had evolved into completely modern bop. His excellent big band made an album and other sides for Musicraft, featuring Dizzy Gillespie and other stars (see historical section). Alto solos w. Barney Bigard on Black & White 12-inch date (*How Long Blues*, etc.) Soprano sax on some Musicraft sides. Three-tenor date w. Coleman Hawkins, Ben Webster on Apollo. Dates w. Billie Holiday, *St. Louis Blues* (Okeh); Sarah Vaughan (Continental).

BILLY BAUER, guitar; b. NYC, Nov. 14, 1915. Started on banjo, mostly self-taught. Joined Jerry Wald on guitar 1939; then with Carl Hoff, Dick Stabile, Abe Lyman, joining Woody Herman early 1944. Since mid-1946, gigs around New York with Chubby Jackson, Lennie Tristano, Benny Goodman. Excellent rhythm man and very modern soloist who has learned much from Tristano. Interesting ideas on his sides with Lennie in Keynote album. Fave: Charlie Christian.

SAUL (SONNY) BERMAN, trumpet; b. 1925. W. Geo. Auld, Harry James, B. Goodman, 1944; Woody Herman, Feb. '45 to late '46. Solos: *Sidewalks of Cuba* w. Woody (Col.); *Curbstone Scuffle, Woodchoppers' Holiday* w. own group and Bill Harris (Dial). One of the most promising young jazzmen, he died of a heart attack Jan. 16, 1947.

DENZIL BEST, drums; b. NYC, 1917. Father played tuba in military band. Piano at 6, trumpet 1940 with Joe Gordon, Chris Columbus. Often sat in on piano, trumpet, at Minton's w. Joe Guy, K. Clarke, Monk. After long illness 1940-41, gigged on piano and bass, took up drums '43. With Saxie Payne, Eddie Williams, Harvey Davis, Leon Gross; nine months w. Ben Webster. Coleman Hawkins, Illinois Jacquet; Sweden with Chubby Jackson, Dec. '47. Comp. *Dee Dee's Dance,* rec. w. Clyde Hart, (Savoy), and Chubby Jackson (Rainbow); *Allen's Alley, Move.* Rec. *Stuffy* w. Hawk (Cap.); pick-up dates w. Vido Musso, Ed Safranski, Helen Humes, Clyde Hart (Savoy), Ben Webster, Al Hall, own group (Wax), Ch. Shavers (Keynote), Mary Lou Williams (Asch), Don Byas (Jamboree), Eddie Davis (Haven), Joe Thomas (HRS), I. Jacquet (Apollo).

ART BLAKEY, drums; b. Pittsburgh, Oct. 11, 1919. Studied piano at school; took up drums by accident when the drummer with a band in which he was playing piano became sick. Joined Fletcher Henderson, 1939; Mary Lou Williams' first band at Kelly's Stable, 1940; then a year w. own group at Tic-Toc in Boston. W. Billy Eckstine for duration of band, 1944-7, then around NYC w. own groups, etc. Rec. w. Eckstine (De Luxe, National), own group, James Moody and Monk (Blue Note). Faves: Max Roach, Sid Catlett, Cozy Cole et al.

NELSON BOYD, bass; b. Camden, N.J., Feb. 6, 1928. Started gigging around Philly 1944. To NY spring 1947. W. Coleman Hawkins at Deuces, w. Tadd Dameron at Onyx. Dexter Gordon at Deuces, Sarah Vaughan in Washington; Dizzy Gillespie, May 1948; Charlie Barnet, Dec. 1948. Rec. *Half Nelson* w. Ch. Parker (Savoy); Six Bips & A Bop (Manor). Faves: Ray Brown, Pettiford. Uses Kay 4-string bass, doesn't like five strings.

JIMMY BLANTON, bass; b. 1919. Studied at Tenn. State College; first prof. break w. Fate Marable, riverboat band pioneer, with whom Duke Ellington discovered him in St. Louis. Joined Duke Oct. '39. First piano-bass duet sides w. Duke were *Blues, Plucked Again* (Col.) Played on all Duke's Victor sides 1940-41 through *Rocks In My Bed, Bli-Blip*. Duet date: *Pitter Panther Patter, Sophisticated Lady, Body & Soul, Mr. J. B. Blues*. Dates w. Cootie Williams (Vocalion), Barney Bigard, Johnny Hodges, Rex Stewart (Bluebird). Was first jazzman to realize full possibilities of bass as a melodic solo instrument, both bowed and plucked; would undoubtedly have been a key figure in bop today and is still idolized by Pettiford and all current bass men. Died Monrovia, Cal., July 30, 1942.

RAY BROWN, bass; b. Pittsburgh, 1926. Studied piano, bass; finished high school 1944; eight months w. Jimmy Hinsley, eight months w. Snookum Russell. Came to NYC, joined Dizzy; rec. w. him small band dates on Dial, Victor, Musicraft, and big band on Musicraft; featured on *One Bass Hit*. Left Dizzy to form own trio which since early 1948 has accompanied his wife, Ella Fitzgerald. Own session on Savoy; trio date w. Dodo Marmarosa (Atomic).

DON CARLOS BYAS, tenor sax; b. Muskogee, Okla., Oct. 21, 1912. Mother played piano, father clarinet. Own group at college, 1930; w. Eddie Barefield in Los Angeles, 1935. Worked w. Don Redman, Lucky Millinder, Eddie Mallory, Andy Kirk, 1939-40, Count Basie 1941, and at Yacht Club w. Coleman Hawkins quintet. Left for Europe, 1946, w. Redman, stayed behind later leading own small groups in Holland, France, etc., and working with French band in Spain. Won Esquire Silver Award 1946. His playing has the big tenor tone, closer to the Hawkins than the Lester Young school; much of his work has the rhythmic and melodic, though not the harmonic, characteristics of bop. Rec. w. Albert Ammons (Commodore), Count Basie *Harvard Blues* etc. (Columbia), Emmett Berry (National), Benny Carter (De Luxe), Cozy Cole (Continental, Guild), Hank d'Amico (National), Leonard Feather (Victor, *Esquire* 12-inch album); Dizzy Gillespie (Manor; Victor 52nd St. album); Johnny Guarnieri (HN Society), Clyde Hart-Rubberlegs Williams-Trummy Young date (Continental), Coleman Hawkins Sax Ensemble (Keynote 12-inch), Cyril Haynes (Comet), Eddie Heywood 12-inch album (Signature), Billie Holiday (Okeh, *I Hear Music* etc.), Pete Johnson-Joe Turner groups (Decca Kansas City album; National); Andy Kirk (Decca); Lips Page (Commodore, Continental, Decca, Savoy); Oscar Pettiford (Manor); Don Redman (Swan); Timme Rosenkrantz (Victor); Mary Lou Williams *Stardust* etc. (Asch 12-inch); Teddy Wilson (Musicraft). Led own recording groups on Savoy, French Blue Star, both of which have Don Byas albums; own dates also on Jamboree, National, Super Disc, American, Arista, Gotham, Hub, French Swing, etc.

GEORGE "RED" CALLENDER, bass. Prominent in Los Angeles since 1937, when he made first record date w. Louis Armstrong. Featured w. Lee &

78

Lester Young 1942; own trio and groups in LA; seen in picture *New Orleans* w. Louis Armstrong, 1947; heard in albums w. Lester Young & King Cole (Aladdin 12-inch); JATP Vol. 1 (Stinson), Andre Previn (Sunset), Charlie Ventura (Black & White 12-inch, Lamplighter), *Just Jazz* (Modern). Comp. *Pastel* rec. w. Erroll Garner (Dial).

CONTE CANDOLI, trumpet; b. Mishawaka, Ind. 1927. Older brother Pete started him on trumpet at 13; played in local groups around South Bend; was only 16 when he joined Woody Herman briefly, then back to high school, graduated January 1945, returned to Woody until drafted; Army Sept. '45-Nov. '46. Spent next year mostly gigging w. Chubby Jackson at Onyx, Deuces, and to Sweden Dec. '47. Stan Kenton, March 1948. Charlie Ventura, Jan. 1949. Solos: *Put That Ring On My Finger* w. Woody (Col.), Chubby Jackson date (Rainbow).

PETE "SUPERMAN" CANDOLI, trumpet; b. Mishawaka, Ind. June 28, 1923. Bass, French horn at 12. Trumpet w. Sonny Dunham, 1940; Will Bradley, '41; Benny Goodman, '42; Ray McKinley, '42; Tommy Dorsey, '43-4; Freddy Slack, Alvino Rey, Ch. Barnet, Teddy Powell, Woody Herman, '44-6; Tex Beneke, '47-8. Many solos with Herman on Col. *Apple Honey,* etc.

SIDNEY ("BIG SID" CATLETT, drums; b. Evansville, Ind. Jan. 17, 1910. School in Chicago; during 1930's played w. Benny Carter, Fletcher Henderson, McKinney's Cotton Pickers, Jeter-Pillars, Don Redman. Louis Armstrong 1938, Benny Goodman, '41, back w. Louis; own group at Three Deuces etc. Joined Louis' small band 1947. Esquire Gold Award, 1944-5. One of most versatile drummers in jazz, fits in with any group from Dixieland to bop. Own boogie-woogie album on Manor; also sessions under own name for Commodore, Super-Disc, Session, Capitol, Delta. Sang own tune *Out of My Way* w. Benny Carter (French Swing). Made *Shaw Nuff, Hot House* w. Diz (Musicraft).

SERGE CHALOFF, baritone sax; b. Boston, Nov. 1923. Father played piano w. Boston Symphony, mother was teacher at New England Conservatory. Took lessons on piano, clarinet, but self-taught on baritone. Listened to Harry Carney and Jack Washington, baritone men with Duke & Count. Joined Tommy Reynolds 1940; then w. Stinky Rogers, Shep Fields, Ina Ray Hutton, Boyd Raeburn. Changed style after hearing Bird, and while with Geo. Auld (1945) and Jimmy Dorsey (1946) evolved as first bop baritone sax man. Joined the new Woody Herman band Sept. 1947. Solos: *Dial-ogue, Blue Serge* (Dial); *Gabardine & Serge, A Bar A Second* (Savoy), *Fine & Dandy, Elevation* w. Red Rodney (Keynote); *Keen and Peachy, Four Brothers* w. Woody (Col.). Great conception and execution, good taste, clean tone and Bird-like style have made him the No. 1 bop exponent of the baritone.

CHARLIE CHRISTIAN, guitar; b. Texas, 1918; died March 2, 1942. Wanted to play tenor sax, but started in music at 12 on his father's guitar. Played bass for Alphonse Trent in Deadwood, S. D. Guitar w. Anna Mae Winburn, Omaha; electric guitar 1937, various groups around Oklahoma, Minnesota and the Dakotas. Joined Benny Goodman July 1939, stayed two years until illness forced his retirement. Further details of his early career in Chapter 1. Rec. all Goodman Sextet sides on Columbia label 1939-41; also *Solo Flight, Honeysuckle Rose* w. Goodman big band (Col.) Two dates w. L. Hampton, featured on *One Sweet Letter From You* (chord style) and *Haven't Named It Yet* (own comp.), both on Victor. *Celestial Express, Profoundly Blue, Edmond Hall Blues, Jammin' In Four* w. Ed Hall (Blue Note 12-inch). *Wrap Your Troubles in Dreams, Star Dust, Old Fashioned Love, Exactly Like You* w. Eddy Howard (Columbia). Ch. Christian Memorial Album recorded at Minton's (Vox). Metronome All Stars, *King Porter, All Star Strut* (Col.), *Bugle Call Rag, One o'Clock Jump* (Victor).

KENNY CLARKE (known as "Klook" or "Kloop"), drums; b. Pittsburgh, Jan. 1914. Father played trombone, brothers drums, bass. Piano, trombone, drums, vibes and theory at high school. Five years w. Leroy Bradley, Roy Eldridge, 1935. To St. Louis w. Jeter-Pillars Orch., to NYC, joined Edgar Hayes, touring with him in Finland, Sweden, 1937; made own quintet date in Stockholm, March 1938, for Odeon, playing vibes and drums. Through Rudy Powell, got job w. Claude Hopkins, stayed eight months, then w. Teddy Hill until break-up. During time with Hill, 1939-40, got to know Dizzy well. Later took remnants of Hill band into Minton's, also worked a few months w. Louis Armstrong; was with Dizzy in Ella Fitzgerald band (when they concocted *Salt Peanuts*) and with Benny Carter, 1941-2. Year and a half in Chicago w. Red Allen; then had own band at Kelly's Stable, NYC, which Coleman Hawkins fronted part of the time. In this band, he and Ike Quebec developed the theme later known as *Mop Mop*. Army 1943 for three years; public relations in London a while; organized and played trombone w. stage band and choral group which played Madeleine Theatre in Paris. Organized Special Service City in Seckenheim, Germany. Joined Dizzy's big band 1946, stayed eight months; since then, mostly with Tadd Dameron, but rejoined Dizzy to make Europeon trip Jan. 1948 and stayed on in Paris a few months making sessions for French Swing record label, teaching, organizing concerts, and training a French band to play bop.

Kenny originally played the old Jo Jones sock cymbal style; later, gradually developed the idea that by using the top cymbal for steady rhythm, he could work out punctuation figures with his foot for bass drum effects, integrating drums with the arrangement and soloists, making drums sound like another instrument instead of just background.

For other details on Kenny, who was a major figure in the birth of bebop, see the historical section. He is heard on the Vox album recorded at Minton's with Charlie Christian and Monk. *Oop Bop Sh'Bam, Our Delight,* etc. with Dizzy (Musicraft); Be Bop Boys (Savoy); own session (Victor bebop album). Comp. *Epistrophy* and other early themes used by boppers.

NAT "KING" COLE, vocal, piano; b. March 17, 1917, Montgomery, Ala. Not a bop artist, but has recorded a couple of pseudo-bop numbers, *That's What* and *The Geek* (Capitol).

WILLIAM (SONNY) CRISS, alto sax; b. Memphis, 1927; to LA 1942. W. Shifty Henry after school hours; finished school winter '46; worked w. Sammy Yates, Johnny Otis, Howard McGhee, Al Killian, and small Eckstine group at Billy Berg's; then w. Gerald Wilson. Joined Norman Granz unit Nov. 1948. Faves: Benny Carter, Ch. Parker. Rec. *The Hunt* and *Bopera* (Bop).

TADLEY EWING (TADD) DAMERON, arranger; b. Cleveland, 1917. Heard parents play piano; jazz rudiments from brother Caesar, who played alto locally. The late Freddy Webster, trumpeter, gave him his professional start as a pianist; then with Zack White, Blanche Calloway. By 1940, in Chicago, had become an arranger, came to NYC with Vido Musso; later joined Harlan Leonard in Kansas City, for whom he wrote many of that band's Bluebird records. After war-plant work, wrote for Lunceford, Basie, Eckstine, Auld, Vaughan; helped organize Babs' Three Bips and a Bop. Wrote *Soulphony* for Dizzy to perform at Carnegie Hall. Led his own quintet at the Royal Roost during most of 1948. Technically weak as a pianist, he is important mainly as one of the first and best arrangers to use the devices of bop, though some of his tunes (*Good Bait, The Chase, Our Delight*) are simple swing melodies, not bop. Best examples of his writing are Dizzy's *Hot House* (Musicraft), *Stay On It, Cool Breeze* (Victor), Auld's *Air Mail Special, 100 Years From Today* (Musicraft), C. Hawkins' *Half Step Down Please* (Victor), but says he has not been well represented on records. Own sessions playing and writing on Savoy and Blue Note; piano & arr. for Sarah Vaughan on Continental (*I'd Rather Have a Memory*), led band on her Musicraft date featuring his own fine ballad, *If You Could See Me Now.* An early student and admirer of bop, Tadd is known as "The Disciple."

MILES DAVIS, trumpet; b. Alton, Ill. 1926; family moved to East St. Louis a year later. Trumpet in high school band. Two years w. Eddie Randall in St. Louis. Father sent him to N. Y. to study at Juilliard, 1945. Joined Ch. Parker, whom he'd met with Eckstine band in St. Louis. W. Coleman Hawkins, Benny Carter; five months w. Eckstine; own band at Royal Roost, Sept. '48, incl. French horn, tuba, alto, tenor, baritone, self and rhythm. Comp. *Becky's Night Out* (rec.

81

by Dave Lambert), *Donna Lee*. Rec. *Little Willie Leaps, Sippin' At Bell's, Milestones*, many other sides w. Bird on Savoy, Dial.

BILL DE ARANGO, guitar; b. Cleveland, Ohio, Sept. 20, 1921. Ohio State U. Local groups 1939-42; Army, '42-44. A year w. Ben Webster around 52nd Street, then own group w. Terry Gibbs in NYC and Chicago; returned to Cleveland 1948. Rec. w. Eddie Davis, Ben Webster (Haven), Ch. Kennedy, Ike Quebec (Savoy), eight sides w. Slam Stewart (Continental), Sarah Vaughan (Continental), Dizzy Gillespie (Victor 52nd St. album). Own session w. Webster, Tony Scott, Leonard Graham, Dense Thornton, John Simmons, Sid Catlett: *Mister Brim, Dark Corners, Jeep Is Jumpin', I Got It Bad* (Haven). Esquire New Star Award, 1946.

BONIFACE FERDINAND LEONARDO (BUDDY) DE FRANCO, clarinet; b. Camden, N. J., Feb. 17, 1923. Son of piano tuner. Clarinet at 12; won prize in Tommy Dorsey amateur contest; jammed at Billy Kretchmer's sessions. Joined Scat Davis late 1939. With Gene Krupa, 1941-2; Ted Fio Rito, '42; Charlie Barnet, '43-4; Tommy Dorsey, '44-6; settled in California, then joined Boyd Raeburn. Back with Dorsey Sept. '47-Sept. '48. Solos: *Opus One, You're Driving Me Crazy* w. Dorsey (Victor); Metronome All Stars' *Look Out* (Victor), *Leap Here* (Capitol). Charlie Shavers sessions (Vogue). Won Down Beat poll as best sideman-clarinetist, 1947-8. Generally rated among musicians as the greatest musician playing modern jazz on this instrument, he is one of the more serious-minded bop men with an interest in composing and in all forms of music.

GENE DI NOVI, piano; b. Brooklyn, 1928; in music business at 14, with Henry Jerome at Childs Restaurant 1943, then Joe Marsala at Hickory House, Boyd Raeburn, Buddy Rich and back with Raeburn. Gigs at Three Deuces, as single and with Chuck Wayne Trio. Benny Goodman Sextet briefly, 1948, then in unit acc. Anita O'Day. Solos: *Slightly Dizzy* w. Marsala (Musicraft); *Sheik of Araby* w. Lester Young (Aladdin); *Aaron's Axe, Tiny's Con* w. Aaron Sachs (Manor). A very promising soloist in the Bud Powell tradition; has also written arrangements for Ch. Ventura.

ALLEN EAGER, tenor sax; b. NYC, 1926. On the road at fifteen with Bobby Sherwood; later w. Sonny Dunham, Woody Herman, Hal McIntyre, Shorty Sherock, T. Dorsey, Johnny Bothwell (small band at Three Deuces) and since 1945 mostly around 52nd Street, including own group at Spotlite; 1948 w. Tadd Dameron at Royal Roost. Rec. own dates for Savoy: *Rampage, Booby Hatch, Vot's Dot, Meeskite* etc. and *O-Go-Mo, Mr. Dues* w. Teddy Reig. Red Rodney date, *Fine and Dandy* (Keynote); *Allen's Alley* in 52nd St. album (Victor); *Deedle*

w. Dave Lambert (Sitting In); WNEW Vol. 2 (Vox). Erratic, but one of the fastest and most exciting tenor men of the Lester Young school when at his best.

BILLY ECKSTINE, valve trombone, vocalist; b. Pittsburgh, 1914. High school and Howard Univ. in Washington, D. C. With Earl Hines 1939-43, singing and playing occasional trumpet; own big band, 1944-6; small band, 1947, then worked as a single. Trombone solos: *Mr. B's Blues* (MGM); *She's Got the Blues For Sale, Long Long Journey, Cool Breeze* (National). As an instrumentalist, has more enthusiasm than technique, but as a bandleader he played an important part in bop history. Full details in Chapter 3.

WALTER GILBERT FULLER, arranger; b. Los Angeles, 1920. Studied at N.Y.U., then returned to the coast, writing for Les Hite (*T Bone Blues, That's the Lick, World Is Waiting for Sunrise* etc.) and Floyd Ray. Came East with Ray 1938, later working for Jimmie Lunceford, Tiny Bradshaw. One of the first arrangers to work in the bop idiom, he wrote for Eckstine, helped to assemble and direct Dizzy Gillespie's band, was co-composer and arranger of *One Bass Hit, Ray's Idea, Things to Come, Ool-Ya-Koo, Manteca, That's Earl Brother,* and the *Swedish Suite* premiered at Carnegie Hall May 1948. *Fuller Bop Man, Tropicana* for James Moody (Blue Note). Has owned several music publishing companies, written arrs. for publishers, and is the author of a bop arranging method published by J. J. Robbins. No relation to the Chicago trumpeter Walter Fuller.

ERROLL GARNER, piano; b. Pittsburgh, June 15, 1921; father also pianist. Has never learned to read music. Local bands at 16. To NYC 1944, 52nd St. jobs at Tondelayo's, Three Deuces; joined Slam Stewart Trio, later formed own trio. Two albums on Mercury, one on Disc; solo sessions for Black & White, Savoy, Dial, Signature, Victor, Rex. Not quite a bopper, but an extremely original modern pianist with highly rhythmic delayed-action right hand on fast tunes, schmaltzy spread-chords style on slow ballads. Sat in w. Geo. Auld band for one session (Musicraft album); also heard on dates under Slam's name (Savoy, Manor), Don Byas (Super Disc, Arista), Ch. Parker *Bird's Nest* etc. (Dial), Just Jazz Album (Modern).

STANLEY GETZ, tenor sax; b. Philly, Feb. 2, 1927. Started on bass in the Bronx, then bassoon; James Monroe High. · W. All City Orch. At 15, joined Dick "Stinky" Rogers until a truant officer yanked him off the job. Started again at 16, w. Jack Teagarden, Dale Jones, Bob Chester; a year with Kenton, few months with Jimmy Dorsey and Benny Goodman (solos on BG's *Swing Angel, Rattle & Roll, Give Me the Simple Life*). While w. BG, made 4 small band sides w. Kai Winding (Savoy). Worked w. Randy Brooks, Buddy Morrow, Herbie Fields, then settled on West coast. W. Butch Stone; own trio at Swing Club, Hollywood. W. Woody Herman's band from its organization, September 1947. Faves: Charlie Parker on tenor; Lester Young, Herbie Steward. Rec. *Opus De Bop* (Savoy); *As I Live and Bop, Interlude in Bebop, Black Magic* (Sitting In); last solo on *Four Brothers* w. Woody (Col.)

TERRY GIBBS (Gubenko), vibes; b. Brooklyn, Oct. 13, 1924. Father played violin, bass, on Jewish radio shows; brother and two sisters all musical. Sneaked in to study on his brother's xylophone when brother not home. Studied drums, tympani, won Major Bowes contest at 12, tourned with Bowes. Back to school. Army, three years. Club dates w. Bill de Arango ("nicest cat I ever worked for"); first rec. w. Allen Eager, *Meeskite* (Savoy). Six weeks w. Tommy Dorsey; Sweden w. Chubby Jackson, Dec. 1947; Buddy Rich to Sept. 1948, then w. Woody Herman. Rec. six sides w. Chubby in Sweden (Rainbow); Aaron Sachs date (Manor). Faves: Milton Jackson, Teddy Cohen. Amazing technique and modern conception make him outstanding modern jazzman on vibes.

JOHN BIRKS "DIZZY" GILLESPIE, trumpet; see Chapter I *et seq.* Biographical details in Chapter III.

DEXTER GORDON, tenor sax; b. Feb. 27, 1923, Los Angeles. Father was doctor whose patients included Duke Ellington, Lionel Hampton. Studied harmony, theory, clarinet at 13; alto at 15. Finished school 1940, took up tenor; Harlem Collegians, local band. W. Lionel Hampton, Dec. 1940, stayed three years. Back to L. A. w. Lee Young, Jesse Price; six months w. Louis Armstrong in '44. First recorded solo was *Blowing the Blues Away* during 18 months with Eckstine band. To N. Y., got 802 card; w. Ch. Parker at Spotlite; own group at Deuces. To West Coast summer 1946; two months in Honolulu w. Cee Pee Johnson. To NY late '47, gigged áround 52nd Street. Rec. w. own groups, Savoy and Dial; Benny Carter (De Luxe), Sir Charles (Apollo), Red Norvo (Cap.), Mary Ann McCall (Col.); *Blue 'N' Boogie*, first small-band Gillespie side (Guild, Musicraft).

WARDELL GRAY, tenor sax; b. Oklahoma City, 1921. One brother, Harry, plays bass. Started on clarinet in Detroit; studied at Cass Tech. Worked with Jimmy Rachel, Benny Carew, joined Earl Hines 1943, playing alto in Earl's big male-and-female band. Stayed with Earl two years, then settled on the West Coast, working with Vernon Alley, Benny Carter, Billy Eckstine's small group, and at Gene Norman jazz concerts. Benny Goodman heard him at one of these concerts and brought him to New York, spring 1948, to work with Goodman Sextet. Worked a few weeks with Count Basie at the Royal Roost before rejoining Benny in the new big Goodman band, November 1948. Says the only record of his own that he likes is *Sweet Georgia Brown* on Modern. Also made *Just Jazz* albums (Modern), *Camarillo* and other sides with Bird on Dial, *This Is It* with J. C.

Heard (Apollo); *The Chase* (two sides) with Dexter Gordon (Dial), and solo session on Sitting In label. Some sides with Hines on ARA. Was rated as best new tenor star of 1948 by Goodman, Lester Young, Teddy Wilson and many other experts.

BENNIE GREEN, trombone; b. Chicago, 1923. Brother Elbert played tenor with Roy Eldridge. High school band and local gigs to 1942, then joined Earl Hines. Drafted Nov. 1943; two years in 343rd Army band, Illinois, six months on coast; discharged May 1946, rejoined Hines, stayed until January 1948, worked briefly with Gene Ammons, then joined Charlie Ventura. Rec. *Euphoria, I'm Forever Blowing Bubbles* with Ventura (National); Six Bips & A Bop (Manor); *Ollopa, This Is It* with J. C. Heard (Apollo). Faves: Tommy Dorsey, Bobby Byrne, J. J. Johnson, Lawrence Brown, Matthew Gee. One of the most original trombone men.

ALAN (AL) HAIG, piano; b. Newark, 1923; raised in Nutley, N. J. Coast Guard bands, 1942-4; out of service March '44, club dates around Boston, worked briefly w. Jerry Wald. Joined Dizzy's quintet May '45, when he made the famous Guild-Musicraft date (Hot House, Shaw Nuff); on coast with Diz, made Dial date, Feb. '46; in NYC, 52nd St. album (Victor). Also rec. while w. Ch. Barnet late '45 (solo on *E Bob O Lee Bob*), (Decca). Dates w. Red Rodney (Keynote), Ben Webster (*Doctor Keets, Spang,* on Haven). Own trio, *Always* (Sitting In). One of first and best pianists to play in strictly bop idiom.

"LITTLE BENNY" HARRIS, trumpet; b. NYC, April 1924; father a full-blooded San Blas Indian; has title to islands, pineapple, chocolate sources etc. but says "I have no eyes for the woods." French horn in Daily Mirror kids' band at 12. Shined shoes; self-taught musician, took up trumpet 1937. Got into music business through Dizzy, whom he met after the Teddy Hill band's return from Paris, 1937. Benny, who was studying aviation then, was recommended by Diz to Tiny Bradshaw, whom he joined in 1939 for six months.

Spent many nights hanging around with Diz at the Savoy; lived with Charlie Parker at the Woodside; joined Earl Hines 1941, later worked with John Kirby, Benny Carter, Herbie Fields, Don Redman, Boyd Raeburn, and with Don Byas at the Three Deuces. First records with Clyde Hart, *Little Benny (Ideology)* and *Dee Dee's Dance,* (Savoy); Don Byas *How High the Moon* (Savoy). Composed *Ornithology* as variation on *How High the Moon.* See references in historical section. Little Benny, a key figure in the evolution of bebop, believes the other main protagonists included Diz, Bird, Monk, Pettiford, Kenny Clarke, Denzil Best.

BILL HARRIS, slide and valve trombone; b. Philadelphia 1916. Was a truck driver for a while, worked in warehouse, read electric meters; studied tenor, trumpet, drums, trombone, jobbed with Ventura, De Franco. Starting seriously on trombone in 1938, worked briefly with Krupa, Ray McKinley, then joined Buddy Williams in Dayton. A year with Bob Chester, then year with Benny Goodman, 1943; settled on West Coast, gigged w. Ch. Barnet, F. Slack. Own sextet at Cafe Society Uptown, spring 1944, w. Zoot Simms, Ernie Figueroa, Clyde Hart, Specs Powell (later Sid Catlett), Sid Weiss; with Joe Bushkin replacing Hart, this group made a Commodore session May 1944. Returned briefly to Bob Chester, then joined Woody Herman Aug. 1944, stayed until band broke up Dec. 1946; small groups w. Charlie Ventura and on own, also tours with Jazz at Phil. Rejoined Herman Oct. 1948. Closer to Dixieland than bop rhythmically, Harris nevertheless gave jazz the newest trombone style since Jack Teagarden rose to fame twenty years earlier. Rec. *Bijou* w. Herman, (Col.) own small band dates (Keynote, Dial); w. Chubby Jackson (Keynote), Flip Phillips (Signature), WNEW Vol. 2 (Vox), Benny Morton four-trombone date (Keynote 12-inch). Intense, emotional style on slow numbers and exciting, choppy rhythmic solos on fast choruses. Began to tend more toward bop during 1948.

AKE (STAN) HASSELGARD, clarinet; b. Bollnas, Sweden, Oct. 4, 1922. Raised in Upsala; clarinet in school band. Rec. w. Simon Brehm, 1942 (Musica), Bob Laine (Cupol), Tyree Glenn (Musica). Got BA degree May '47 and came to U. S. July to take course at Columbia U. in history of art. Later went to Hollywood, where Benny Goodman heard him at a jam session and hired him. Worked NYC and Philly w. Benny; own quintet at Three Deuces. Killed Nov. 23 1948 in automobile accident, Decatur, Ill. American recordings w. own group: *Swedish Pastry, Who Sleeps; I'll Never Be the Same, Sweet and Hot Mop* (Capitol). Was developing rapidly into one of the foremost bop-influenced clarinetists.

COLEMAN HAWKINS, tenor sax; b. St. Joseph, Mo., Nov. 21, 1904. Piano, 'cello at five; tenor at nine; Washburn College, Topeka. Mamie Smith's Jazz Hounds, Kansas City, 1922; Fletcher Henderson, 1924-34; England with Jack Hylton and Mrs. Jack Hylton bands, 1934-5; Holland, France, Belgium, Scandanavia with own groups until July 1939; back in NYC, own nine-piece band at Kelly's Stable which recorded *Body and Soul* for Bluebird, Oct. 11, 1939. Own big band at Golden Gate Ballroom and Fiesta Danceteria, 1939-40; since then, has worked as a single or with own small bands, and toured several times with Granz's Jazz at Philharmonic. Organized first bop record session, Feb. 1944 (Apollo)— details in Chapter 3. From 1944 on, men on his night club engagements and record dates included Dizzy, Howard McGhee, Fats Navarro, Miles Davis, J. J. Johnson, Kai Winding, Milt Jackson, Sir Charles, Monk, Curly Russell, Oscar Pettiford, Max Roach, Denzil Best et al. His own work, though not strictly bop, has long featured double-time and other effects that have been incorporated into bop. There are Hawkins albums on Joe Davis and Asch labels; as Gold Award Esquire winner four straight years, he appeared in both Esquire albums on Victor, also 52nd St. Jazz and Bebop albums (Victor), and in two tenor sax albums on Savoy, one on Keynote, one Decca. His bop singles include *Stuffy* (Capitol), *I Mean You* (Sonora), *Salt Peanuts* co-starred with Geo. Auld, Ben Webster (Apollo). First to popularize tenor sax in jazz, still the greatest all-around artist on this instrument in 1949.

NEAL HEFTI, arranger and trumpet; b. Hastings, Neb., Oct. 29, 1922. Six months with Bob Astor around New Jersey, 1941; to Cuba with Les Lieber, 1942; with Bobby Byrne, Charlie Barnet, Charlie Spivak. Joined Woody Herman late 1944. Married Frances Wayne, then Woody's vocalist; settled in Los Angeles with her and has written for Ziggy Elman, Barnet and many other bands. One of the first musicians from downtown to dig the developments at Minton's, Neal was playing and writing bop around 1943. Best numbers include *Wildroot, The Good Earth* for Woody (Columbia), *Mo Mo* for George Auld (Musicraft), *Sloppy Joe's* and *I Woke Up Dizzy* by his own small bop group in Keynote album. Played on Metronome and Esquire All Star dates for Victor; solo and arrangement on *Some of These Days* w. Benny Carter (De Luxe); Chubby Jackson (Queen), Flip Phillips (Signature), also played and arranged for big Charlie Ventura band, *Misirlou, How High The Moon*, etc. Sept. 1946 (National). Scored *Frustration, Everything Happens To Me* for Bill Harris (Keynote).

WOODROW CHARLES HERMAN, bandleader; b. May 16, 1913, Milwaukee. Woody makes no claim to being a modern jazz soloist; his work on clarinet and alto, which he has confined to occasional short solos in recent years, definitely has no relationship with bop, though his bands, especially the one formed in 1947, have been rated by many critics as the greatest large bop group in jazz. For details of the Herman orchestra history, see Chapter 5.

GREIG STEWART "CHUBBY" "SLIM" JACKSON, bass; b. NYC, Oct. 25, 1918. Has lived most of life in Freeport, L. I. Mother is veteran vaudevillian and pianist, still active locally. Clarinet in high school band at 15. Started on bass at 16. Studied at Ohio State U. and with Homer Mensch of NY Phil. Mike Riley, 1937; Johnny Messner, 1938; Raymond Scott, 1939; Jan Savitt, 1940; Terry Shand, Henry Busse, 1941; Charlie Barnet, 1941-3; Woody Herman, 1943-46; small group with Charlie Ventura, then own small groups, one of which he took to Sweden, December 1947. Rejoined Woody Herman summer 1948. In addition to his bass work, Chubby has earned fame through his comedy personality, his beards, five-string bass, amplifier, reducing diets, flowing bow ties, Jewish dialect, etc., and through the spirit he instils into every group with which he works. Won Esquire New Star Award 1945 and Gold Star Award '46 and '47; played in both Esquire All Star albums (Victor). Own sessions on Queen, Keynote; Herman Woodchoppers album (Columbia); session cut in Sweden (Rainbow).

MILTON JACKSON, vibraharp; b. Detroit, 1923. Music course at Mich. State; local bands, 1942, until Dizzy heard him and brought him to NYC, 1945. Dates w. Diz on Dial, Victor (52nd St. album) and Musicraft (*Things to Come, That's Earl Brother,* etc.), Dinah Washington date on Apollo; Be Bop Boys (Savoy); Coleman Hawkins (Sonora); Thel. Monk (Blue Note). First vibes star to play bop; since leaving Diz, has worked w. Howard McGhee, Tadd Dameron and own small groups around New York.

BATTISTE ILLINOIS JACQUET, tenor sax; b. Houston, Oct. 30, 1921. Father played bass in railroad company band. Soprano sax, 1943. W. Lionel Proctor; alto, two years w. Bob Cooper; Milton Larkins band; to coast w. Floyd Ray, tenor w. Lionel Hampton, 1941, where he became famous through his much-imitated solo on Flying Home (Decca). Cab Calloway, 1943-4; Basie, '45-6; toured with Granz, formed own band, became one of highest-priced jazz soloists in the country, featured with Ed Sullivan at Roxy and on television, etc. Although famous for his freak high notes and other audience-courting showmanship stunts rather than for any musical accomplishments, Jacquet has at times shown that he can play modern tenor in good taste, e.g., The King, *Mutton Leg* with Basie; *Memories of You, Robbins Nest* with own group (Apollo); *Illinois Blows the Blues* and his own ballad *You Left Me All Alone* (Aladdin); *Riffin' at 24th St.* (Victor). He can also be heard in his own album on Savoy; in Vols. I, IV, V, etc. of Jazz at the Philharmonic (Asch & Disc); in Sid Catlett, Al Casey dates (Capitol) and King Cole Quintet album (Disc). Seen in Warner Bros. short *Jammin' The Blues.*

ALBERT (BUDD) JOHNSON, tenor sax and arranger; b. Dallas, 1910. Drums at 7; studied music with Booker T. Washington's daughter. On the road at 14, playing drums. Took up tenor 1926; to Kansas City 1927; worked with Geo. E. Lee; had small group in Chicago with Teddy Wilson until they both joined Louis Armstrong, 1933. With Earl Hines on and off from Sept. 1934 to Christmas 1942; during that time also worked with Fletcher and Horace Henderson. Then with John Kirby; U.S.O. tour with Al Sears, Lester Young. Own band with Dizzy at Onyx and Yacht Clubs, then with Roy at Onyx and with Pettiford at Yacht. Arrangements for Jerry Jerome NBC orchestra. Own group at Three Deuces. Replaced Dizzy as leader of first Eckstine band. 1946, joined J. C. Heard at Cafe Society. Free lancing 1948, with Buster Harding and other location band in New York City. Led a new band briefly for Hines, December 1948. Wrote almost all the Billy Eckstine arrangements in the Hines band. Solos on *Skylark, Swamplands. Blue and Sentimental* with Leslie Scott (Victor); alto solo with Coleman Hawkins on *Jumping for Jane* (Victor, bebop album); tenor with Heard (Continental), Clyde Hart (Savoy), Pete Johnson (National), Kirby (Asch), Dickie Wells (HRS); sat in on dates with Lionel Hampton, Woody Herman.

JAMES LOUIS JOHNSON, trombone; b. Indianapolis, Jan. 1924. Piano at 11, trombone at 14. Clarence Love, Sept. 1941-Feb. '42; Snookum Russell, March-Oct. '42; Benny Carter to '45; Count Basie, '45-6; bop quintet at Spotlite w. Allen Eager, '46; inactive for eight months 1947, then joined Illinois Jacquet. Solos: *The King, Bambo,* etc. with Basie (Columbia); *Love For Sale* w. Carter (Capitol); *Indiana Winter* w. Esquire All Stars after winning New Star award, Dec. 1946 (Victor album); dates w. Karl George (Melodisc); Coleman Hawkins *Bean & The Boys, I Mean You* (Sonora); Hawkins' date in Victor bebop album; Jazz at Phil. Vol. IV (Disc). Several sessions on Savoy incl. own date, *Mad Be Bop, Jay Bird, Jay Jay, Coppin' The Bop;* Leo Parker date, *Wee Dot,* etc. Solos w. Jacquet on Victor incl. *Mutton Leg.* Certainly the fastest and most inspired bop trombonist, the pace-setter for the new style on this instrument, with technique so phenomenal that listeners to records frequently believe he must be playing a valve trombone.

HENRY "HANK" JONES, piano and arranger; b. Pontiac, Mich. 1918. Brother Thad plays trumpet, other brothers play piano, drums. Studied piano with Carlotta Franzell, who played Cindy Lou in *Carmen Jones.* W. Benny Carew in Lansing (Lucky Thompson, Wardell Gray were in this band); Cleveland w. Tommy Enoch; Buffalo w. Geo. Clarke, then to NYC and through Lucky got a job with Lips Page at Onyx. Five months w. Andy Kirk; briefly w. Eckstine; six months w. John Kirby; two years on and off w. Coleman Hawkins, also at Three Deuces w. various groups under Budd Johnson, Ch. Shavers, Bill Harris, Howard McGhee and Lucky. JATP tour fall of '47. Rock Island, Ill. w. Louis Bellson-Shavers group, spring '48. Joined Ella Fitzgerald as accompanist April '48, went with her to. England fall '48. First rec. *The Lady in Bed* w. Lips (Continental, Nov. 1944). Comp. *Ripples* (rec. w. Kirby in Crown album); *Bean-a-Re-Bop, Angel Face* (rec. by Hawkins on Aladdin, Victor); *Opus De Bop* (rec. w. Be Bop Boys on Savoy). Other dates w. Hawkins on Ca-Song, Sonora; Leo Parker, J. J. Johnson, Ray Brown sessions (Savoy); Ch. Parker (Clef); Cousin Joe (Gotham); *How High The Moon,* etc. with Ella (Decca); JATP *Perdido* album (Clef); own album of piano solos on Clef, which, as he points out, is wrongly titled "Hank Jones' Be Bop Piano." Hank can play bebop, and does on most of his band dates, but in this solo album he plays modern jazz without any bop characteristics.

NORMAN "TINY" KAHN, drums; b. NYC, 1924. Harmonica at six; won prize playing it before La Guardia in Central Park Mall. Drums at 15; tympani in Tilden High Symphony. Professional job in group acc. Judy Kane; bands incl. Milt Britton, Geo. Auld, Boyd Raeburn, Red Rodney, subbed w. Buddy Rich. In addition to drumming, is a self-taught arranger of great talent; originals incl. *Cent and a Half* rec. Lambert & Stewart (Keynote); *Gabardine & Serge* rec. Chaloff (Savoy), *So Long Joe* for Buddy Rich, *Three Cents Plain* for Woody Herman.

BERNARD (BARNEY) KESSEL, guitar; b. Muskogee, Okla. (Don Byas' home town), Oct. 17, 1924, next to youngest of six children in non-musical family. Sold papers as a child; at 13, saw a guitar in a hockshop window and bought it for $1. Never studied music at all. At 16, went to Los Angeles. Ben Pollack called his number, looking for a guitarist who'd lived there previously; instead, Kessel got the job, in Chico Marx's band, which Pollack was organizing. Stayed with Marx nine months; the band included Marty Napoleon, Marty Marsala and Geo. Wettling. Jobbed in Los Angeles 1943, joined Artie Shaw 1944 and stayed a year; featured on Gramercy Five records with Dodo, Roy Eldridge (Victor). Worked around L.A. with Hal McIntyre, Charlie Barnet. Toured with Norman Granz unit including Bird, Sarah Vaughan, 1948. Faves: Charlie Christian, Herb Ellis, Jim Rainey, Mundell Lowe, Chuck Wayne, many others. Records: four sides under own name on Atomic. Capitol dates with B. Goodman (no solos), Red Norvo, Stan Hasselgard. Lucky Thompson (Victor bop album). Ch. Parker's Cheers, Camarillo, Carving the Bird, Stupendous (Dial). Ch. Ventura Lamplighter album. One solo side on The Hunt (Bop). One of the fastest and most musicianly of bop guitarists. Seen in Norman Granz film *Jammin' The Blues*.

LEE KONITZ, alto sax; b. Chicago, 1927. Started on clarinet. Tenor with Gay Claridge at Chez Paree for one month, then with Teddy Powell, 1942; two days after joining latter, leader was arrested and band broke up. Switched to alto to join a society band. Few months w. Jerry Wald, then studied at Roosevelt College. Claude Thornhill, August 1947; solos on *Anthropology*, *Yardbird Suite* (Columbia). With Miles Davis' nine-piece group at Royal Roost, Sept. 1948; then study and gigs w. Lennie Tristano. One of the few bop alto men to have found an individual style instead of copying Bird.

DON LAMOND, drums; b. Oklahoma City, Aug. 18, 1941, son of a lawyer. Raised in Washington, studied all percussion instr. at Peabody Inst. in Balto. W. Rodd Raffell 1940; Sonny Dunham, Boyd Raeburn to Oct. '44; own combo in Washington 1945, then replaced Dave Tough in Herman band till its break-up late 1946. Joined new Herman band Sept. 1947. A great modern

One of the first and foremost figures in the bop movement,
"LITTLE BENNY" HARRIS.

:NNY GREEN with CHARLIE VENTURA at the Royal Roost.

A Herman Leonard shot of EARL "BUD
POWELL at a Royal Roost jam session

Tenor sax man DEXTER GORDON an
valve trombonist BILLY ECKSTINE wit
Billy's band at a National recording dat
1945.

The gentleman from Key West—THEODORE "FATS" NAVARRO
Picture by Herman Leonard.

rombonist J. J. JOHNSON at a bop session conducted by the
ithor (left) at the Royal Roost for a WMGM broadcast,
December 1948.

This close-up of CECIL PAYNE is typical of the brilliant work of Herman Leonard, New York's official photographer to the bop movement.

Two more Herman Leonard shots taken at a WMGM bop session from the Royal Roost. BUDDY DE FRANCO, No. 1 bop clarinetist, and BARBARA CARROLL, a young star from Worcester, Mass. regarded as the leading feminine exponent of bop piano.

HOWARD McGHEE and OSCAR PETT
FORD with the Charlie Barnet orchestr
of 1943.

drummer, heard to advantage on most of Woody's Columbia sides from Nov. 1945 on, also Just Jazz Album (Modern).

STAN LEVEY, drums; b. Philly, 1925. Studied piano and arranging at high school. Met Dizzy at the Down Beat in Philly, 1942, when Diz had a quartet there; worked briefly with him, then came to New York at the suggestion of Bama Warwick; joined Oscar Pettiford at the Onyx. Met Bird at the Down Beat; worked around 52nd Street with Bird, with Barney Bigard at the Onyx, and in the quintet featuring both Diz and Bird which made bop history, 1945. Also worked for Woody Herman, Geo. Auld, then back to Bird; with Ventura's big band, back again to Bird; Three Deuces with Allen Eager, Geo. Shearing, other groups. Joined Freddy Slack, 1948. First records with Barney Bigard, Etta Jones on Black & White, Dec. 1944. Six Dial sides with Dizzy; Lambert-Stewart date (Keynote); session with Eager (Savoy). Fave: Max Roach.

JOHN AARON LEWIS, arranger, piano; b. LaGrange, Ill. 1920, but lived in New Mexico from age of two months. Father an optician; mother studied singing with daughter of Mme. Schumann-Heink. Piano at 7, school in Albuquerque. Majored in anthropology and music at Univ. of New Mexico, 1942, then into Army until Nov. 1945. To NYC Christmas '45; Kenny Clarke, whom he'd met in the Army, introduced him to Dizzy. Wrote vocal arrs. for Kenny Hagood, also *Two Bass Hit* feat. Ray Brown. First major work, *Toccata for Trumpet and orchestra*, priemiered by Dizzy at Carnegie Hall, Sept. 1947. Piano w. Dizzy, June '46-April '48; w. Ill. Jacquet, Oct. '48. Twelve sides playing piano on Savoy small-band dates w. Ch. Parker, Miles Davis; solos w. Diz on *Emanon* (Musicraft), *Stay On It, Minor Walk* (Victor). One of the brightest minds ever applied to bebop.

SHELDON (SHELLY) MANNE, drums; b. NYC, 1921. W. Raymond Scott, Bobby Byrne, Les Brown, Benny Goodman; three years in Coast Guard. At Three Deuces w. Johnny Bothwell Sextet, then to Stan Kenton; featured on *Artistry in Percussion,* etc. Left Kenton, 1948, for few months; w. Geo. Shearing at Deuces, then own group in Chicago; rejoined Kenton late '48. 52nd. St. All Stars date in Victor album. First records w. Joe Marsala, May 1941, Bull's Eye, Lower Register, etc. (Decca). Many small-band dates from 1943, with Flip Phillips, Barney Bigard, Coleman Hawkins, Eddie Heywood album, all Signature; Dizzy Gillespie, Oscar Pettiford (Manor); Kai Winding, Teddy Reig (Savoy), Jimmy Jones, Sandy Williams (HRS), Boyd Raeburn (Musicraft). Excellent all-around drummer with big fan following.

MICHAEL (DODO) MARMAROSA, piano; b. Pittsburgh, 1926. Went to school with Erroll Garner; used to sneak out of classes to hold piano sessions with him. From 1940 to '44, played with the same bands as Buddy de Franco, starting with Scat Davis, then Gene Krupa, Ted Fio Rito, Charlie Barnet, Tommy Dorsey. With Artie Shaw, 1944-5. Settling in California, gigged with Boyd Raeburn, Tommy Pederson, Lucky Thompson. *Skyliner*, etc. with Barnet (Decca), Gramercy 5 sides with Shaw. Countless pick-up band dates in L.A. Best solo sides: *Mellow Mood* (Atomic), *Trade Winds* (Dial). Dates with Ch. Parker, Howard McGhee (Dial), Slim Gaillard (Atomic, Cadet, Melodisc, Four Star, Majestic, etc.), Lucky Thompson (Victor, Down Beat), Barney Kessel (Atomic), Red Norvo (Capitol), Lem Davis (Sunset), Lester Young on *D.B. Blues* date (Aladdin), Raeburn sessions on Jewel. Probably the most gifted technically, as well as the most versatile of all bop pianists.

HOWARD McGHEE, trumpet; b. Tulsa, Okla., March 6, 1918. Father was a doctor; a brother, now deceased, played guitar and taught Howard chords. Family moved to Detroit 1921. Clarinet in high school band; switched to trumpet after hearing Louis Armstrong at the Graystone Ballroom. Had own twelve-piece band at Club Congo. Joined Lionel Hampton, 1941, for three months; then to Andy Kirk, with whom he recorded his own comp. & arr. *McGhee Special* and his arr. of *Hip Hip Hooray*, July 1942. Joined Charlie Barnet, August 1942, for a year, then back with Kirk until mid-1944. Worked briefly with first Eckstine band, also two weeks with Basie. With Georgie Auld in band that also included Al Cohen, Sonny Berman and Shadow Wilson. With Coleman Hawkins at Down Beat and in California; made Capitol session with Hawk, also Asch album. Three years in Cal. mostly with various small groups of his own; toured with Norman Granz; formed own big band late 1948. Not identified with a bop style until 1944, he is now the best known trumpet exponent of bop after Dizzy. Made numerous West Coast dates under own name on Dial, Aladdin (Philo), Modern Music, Melodisc, etc. Also featured on dates with Chubby Jackson (*Crying Sands,* Keynote), Slim Gaillard (20th Century, Majestic, Bel-Tone), Charlie Parker (*Cheers,* etc., Dial), Willie Smith, Charlie Ventura (Sunset), *Oodie Coo Bop* session and Junior Jazz album (Black & White), Jazz at Philharmonic Vol. I (Stinson-Asch), Just Jazz Album (Modern). Own date in Paris, May 1948, on Swing label, while participating in all-star French jazz festival.

ALFRED McKIBBON, bass; b. Chicago, 1919. Raised in Detroit; w. local bands incl. Kelly Martin, Ted Buckner. To NYC 1943 w. Lucky Millinder, then w. Tab Smith, a year w. Coleman Hawkins. 1946-7 w. brother-in-law J. C. Heard's sextet. Joined Dizzy Gillespie, 1947, played on Victor sides incl. *Two Bass Hit, Ow!* Made European tour w. Diz. Various 52nd St. groups, 1948; concerts w. Norman Granz; rejoined Diz Nov. '48. Dates w. J. C. Heard. Ethel Waters (Continental); Dickie Wells, Buck Clayton (HRS), 52nd St. album (Victor). Big, clean tone; excellent rhythm and solo man.

THELONIOUS SPHERE MONK, arranger; b. NYC, 1919. See references in Chapter I *et seq.* Records w. Charlie Christian (Vox album), own groups (Blue Note), Coleman Hawkins (Joe Davis album).

OSCAR MOORE, guitar; b. Austin, Texas, Dec. 25, 1916. School in Phoenix, Ariz.; guitar at 6; music w. private teachers; first pro. date w. brother Johnny, 1934. Joined King Cole, Sept. 1937, left him ten years later to join brother Johnny's Three Blazers. Solos on many Cole records (Decca, Capitol), also Tatum-Joe Turner sides (Decca); eight sides w. L. Hampton, 1940 (Victor). Esquire Gold Award winner, Down Beat and Metronome awards.

THEODORE "FATS" NAVARRO, JR., trumpet; b. Key West, Sept. 24, 1923. Third cousin of Charlie Shavers. Father a barber; most of family musical. Finished school in Key West, 1941 after studying piano privately from age of six and trumpet at 13. Also played tenor sax during school vacation, 1939, in Walter Johnson's band in Miami. Two years on trumpet with Snookum Russell (band also included J. J. Johnson); joined Andy Kirk late 1943, took a couple of plunger solos on Decca. Like Dizzy, Fats evolved from a Roy Eldridge-inspired style into bebop. Worked with Billy Eckstine, then settled in N. Y., played with Coleman Hawkins, Tommy Reynolds, various 52nd Street groups, briefly with Illinois Jacquet and Lionel Hampton. Most of 1948 with Tadd Dameron. Solos: *Tell Me Pretty Baby, Without a Song, Long Long Journey* with Eckstine (National); *Eb Pob* and other sides by Be Bop Boys (Savoy); Kenny Clarke date (Victor bebop album and French Swing); C. Hawkins (Victor, Sonora); Jacquet big band date (Aladdin) under name of "Slim Romero;" Tadd Dameron dates (Savoy, Blue Note); WNEW, Vol. 2 (Vox); Benny Goodman *Stealing Apples* (in Capitol *Giants of Jazz* album). Comp. *Ice Freezes Red, Fat Boy, Fat Girl.* Cleanest execution and purest tone of all the newer bop trumpet men.

REMO PALMIERI, guitar; b. NYC, March 29, 1923. Studied guitar and bass. W. Nat Jaffe, Coleman Hawkins, both at Kelly's Stable, 1943, then Red Norvo; radio show w. Mildred Bailey; since then, house man w. Archie Bleyer on Arthur Godfrey show, etc. Rec. *Groovin' High* and *All The Things You Are* w. Dizzy (Musicraft); Esquire All-Star album (Victor 12-inch) after winning Silver Award, 1946; album on non-electric guitar w. Barney Bigard (Rex); *Esquire Stomp* w. L. Feather (Continental); Nat Jaffe Trio date (Black & White 12-inch); Norvo Sextet (Keynote 12-inch); acc. Linda Keene on *I Must Have That Man* (Black & White); Sarah Vaughan *September Song* (Musicraft). Took up tenor sax, 1948.

CHARLES PARKER, alto & tenor sax; see Chapter II *et seq.*

93

LEO PARKER, baritone sax; b. Washington, 1925. Studied alto at high school, but "learned to blow from Charlie Parker." W. Billy Eckstine, Benny Carter, Illinois Jacquet; with the release of Sir Charles Thompson's record of *Mad Lad* (Apollo), featuring Leo throughout, he became known as the most exciting of modern baritone men, with an appeal similar to Jacquet's on tenor. Featured in the "Parkers" album on Savoy (three sides each by himself and Charlie, who is no relation). Inactive owing to illness, 1948. Solos: *Eb-Pob, Ice Freezes Red* w. Fats Navarro (Savoy); *El Sino, Solitude, Senor Leo,* etc. w. own group (Savoy); *Jivin' with Jack the Bellboy* w. Jacquet (Aladdin); *Blowin' Red's Bop* w. Gene Ammons (Aladdin). Tendency to exhibitionism mars many solos, but basically has a good bop style and big tone.

ARTHUR EDWARD (ART) PEPPER, alto sax; b. Gardena, Cal., 1925. Clarinet at 9, alto at 13; private teacher. 1943 w. Gus Arnheim, Lee Young, Benny Carter around LA. Stan Kenton, Nov. '43. Army, Feb. '44-May '46. Free-lanced in Cal. to Sept. '47, then rejoined Kenton. Solos: *Unison Riff, How High The Moon* w. Kenton (Capitol); *Safrantic, Jumping For Jane* w. Safranski (Atlantic).

OSCAR PETTIFORD, bass; b. Okmulgee, Okla., Sept. 30, 1922. Father, Harry Pettiford, Sr., gave up practice of medicine to form a family band featuring his eleven children. Oscar, living in Minneapolis from 1925, started on piano at ten, taught himself bass in 1936, toured the south and middle west with his father, sisters and brothers until 1941. While at Curly's Cafe in Minneapolis, was heard by members of Charlie Barnet band. Joined Barnet January 1943, making two-bass team with Chubby Jackson; left May' 43, hung around Minton's, worked with Roy Eldridge at Onyx; helped to bring bebop to 52nd St. with a group he and Dizzy co-led (details in historical section) and later with his own group, at the Spotlite, Yacht Club, Onyx and Three Deuces. Won Esquire Gold Award and made first records with Leonard Feather's All Stars, Dec. 4, 1943 (Commodore). With Boyd Raeburn, 1945 (recorded *Night in Tunisia,* Musicraft); own trio in San Diego, October '45; joined Duke Ellington Nov. 10, '45, left him Mar. 11, 1948; own trio with Erroll Garner, later with George Shearing, at Three Deuces; all star band at Royal Roost with Garner, Lucky Thompson, Bill Harris, Red Rodney. Many small band dates 1944-6 with Dizzy (Manor, Columbia), Clyde Hart (Regis, Manor), Sonny Greer, Earl Hines, Betty Roche (Apollo), Coleman Hawkins (Signature, Capitol), Ike Quebec (Blue Note), Leonard Feather (Continental), Ben Webster, Helen Humes (Savoy). Led own bands accompanying blues singers Rubberlegs Williams (Manor), Estelle Edson (Black & White), Wynonie Harris (Apollo). Best solos: *The Man I Love* w. Hawkins (Signature 12-inch); *Suddenly It Jumped* w. Ellington (Victor). Probably the

94

most phenomenal bassist since Blanton's death; helped establish this as a real bop solo instrument. Joined Woody Herman, Feb. 1949.

"FLIP" PHILLIPS (Joseph Edward Fillippelli), tenor sax, b. Brooklyn, 1915. Originally better known as clarinetist; Schneider's Lobster House, Brooklyn, 1934-9; Frankie Newton at Kelly's Stable, 1940-41; switched to tenor w. Larry Bennett at Hickory House, 1942-3. Woody Herman 1944-6, then own groups and tours with Jazz at Philharmonic. A modern soloist, not strictly bop; since 1947, noted for freak-note effects a la Jacquet. Several dates under own name for Signature, Mercury, etc. Best solos: *With Someone New* with Woody (Columbia), *Sweet and Lovely* (own Signature 12-inch side).

TOMMY POTTER, bass; b. Philly., 1918, raised Cape May, N.J. Studied piano, guitar, Jersey City; bass in 1940. Worked w. Johnny Malachi in Washington; to Chicago & NY w. Trummy Young. Two years w. Eckstine. Settling in NYC, worked w. John Hardee, Max Roach; mainly w. Ch. Parker since May 1947. Rec. *Rhythm In a Riff* w. Eckstine, *Don't Blame Me* and *Bird Gets the Worm* w. Parker. Faves: Oscar Pettiford, Ray Brown, Ch. Mingus.

EARL (BUDDY) POWELL, piano; b. NYC, 1924. Father, William Powell, and grandfather were musicians; also brother William in Detroit, composer, trumpeter and violinist. Bud quit school at 15, gigged around Coney Island, worked at Canada Lee's Chicken Coop uptown and with Valaida Snow and the Sunset Royals; hung around Minton's during bop's formative era. Spent about three years with Cootie Williams, making all 1944-5 records on Hit, Majestic, Capitol, including the *Echoes of Harlem* album on Hit in which he can be heard playing almost the same bop style he features today. Later with John Kirby at Cafe Society, briefly with Dizzy's small band, and in Town Hall concert with Diz; 52nd Street jobs with Don Byas, Sid Catlett, Allen Eager. Solos: *Chasing The Bird* with Ch. Parker (Savoy), *Jay Bird* with J. J. Johnson (Savoy), Kenny Clarke date (Victor bop album); various Savoy sessions with Dexter Gordon, Fats Navarro (*Webb City, Fat Boy*), etc. and *Reverse Charges* with Frankie Socolow on Duke. One of the first and greatest of bop pianists; was out of circulation throughout 1948 following nervous breakdown.

MAXWELL ROACH, drums; b. Brooklyn, 1924. Finished school 1942, worked at Monroe's Uptown House w. Bird. Like Shelly Manne, Mickey Scrima and other young drummers, he would hang around Kenny Clarke, who was working at Kelly's, but at first Max was so young they wouldn't let him in. Clarke was his basic influence. First rec. w. Coleman Hawkins, Feb. 1944 (Apollo). Six months w. Dizzy's first 52nd St. group; to coast w. Benny Carter (Capitol rec.), then back w. Diz & Bird at Deuces. When Diz left for Coast, Max free-lanced around NYC, with Hawk, Eager *et al* at Spotlite. Most of 1947-8 w. Bird, Tadd Dameron. Dozens of small band dates for Savoy, Dial, etc. Comp. *Coppin' The Bop* (rec. w. J. J. Johnson, Savoy). Greatest of all young bop drummers and idol of his rivals.

ROBERT (RED) RODNEY, trumpet, b. Philly, Sept. 27, 1927. Played drums and bugle in drum corps for Boy Scouts. Trumpet at 13. Massbaum Music School (Buddy De Franco there too); worked w. Alex Bartha in Atlantic City while still at school. On the road at 15; worked with Jerry Wald; Jimmy Dorsey, Tony Pastor, Les Brown, Georgie Auld, Claude Thornhill, Gene Krupa; joined Woody Herman Nov. 1948. Harry James-style solo w. J. Dorsey on *Oh What a Beautiful Morning*. Bop solos w. Krupa: *Just a Matter of Opinion; Just the Other Day; How High The Moon* (Col.) *Yardbird Suite* w. Thornhill (Col.) Serge Chaloff date (Savoy); own small band date (Keynote) and backing Lambert-Stewart bop vocal sides (Keynote). Sat in w. Buddy Rich, solo on *Oop Bop sh'Bam* (Mercury).

MILTON "SHORTY" ROGERS, arranger and trumpet; b. Great Barrington, Mass., April 14, 1924. Classical training at High School of Music & Art, NYC. Leaving school, worked four months with Will Bradley; w. Red Norvo 1942, then Army until Sept. '45, when he joined Woody Herman. Rejoined Woody in new band late 1947 after free-lancing a while. Rec. Kai Winding date (Savoy), Benny Carter all star session (De Luxe), Fan It, Steps, etc. w. Woody. Arr. *Keen and Peachy* for Woody, *Bop!* for Red Norvo (Capitol) and many small band sides by Bill Harris (Dial) and other dates by Herman sidemen. One of the most original young stars both in his writing and his playing.

DILLON "CURLY" RUSSELL, bass; b. NYC, Mar. 19, 1920. Trombone & bass, YMCA Junior Symphony. On the road at 18; w. Don Redman, 1941. To Coast w. Benny Carter; first records w. Benny Oct. 1943, Frisco. NYC w. Harlem Highlanders, trios, etc. and w. Diz & Bird at Deuces. Since 1945, has worked with almost every small group on 52nd St. and at Royal Roost; dates w. Diz, Bird, Dexter Gordon, Coleman Hawkins, Stan Getz, Sarah Vaughan, etc. Seldom takes solos, but fine rhythm man.

AARON SACHS, clarinet; b. NYC, July 4, 1923. Babe Russin, 1941; Red Norvo, '41-2; Van Alexander, '42-3; back with Norvo, '43-4; won Esquire New Star award, '45; w. Benny Goodman, 1945. Solos: *Sarcastic Lady* in Eddie Heywood album (Signature 12-inch); *Gee Ain't I Good To You* w. Linda Keene (Black & White); *No Smokes Blues* w. Sarah Vaughan & Dizzy (Continental); *I Got Rhythm*, etc. w. Red Norvo (Keynote 12-inch); also sessions with Mildred Bailey (Crown); Flip Phillips (Signature), Cozy Cole (Keynote). Own date,

96

1947: *Aaron's Axe, Tiny's Con* (Manor). Inactive owing to illness most of 1948. One of the first to play bop on clarinet.

ED SAFRANSKI, bass; b. Pittsburgh, 1919; father an artist. Violin at 8, switched to bass in high school. Two years Carnegie Tech. On road w. Marty Gregor, 1937, then local bands and arranging for radio. Hal McIntyre, Oct. '41-May '45; w. Miff Mole at Nick's, then to Kenton July '45. Rec. Swanee River, Commando's Serenade w. McIntyre (Victor); Safranski w. Kenton (Capitol); *Experiment Perilous* w. Willie Smith (Sunset); *Pom Pom* w. Cliff Lange (Pan-American); WNEW Vol. I (Vox); eight sides w. Don Byas (Jamboree); dates w. Vido Musso and own group (Savoy); *Turmoil, Safrantic, Bass Mood, Jumping for Jane* with own septet from Kenton band, 1947 (Atlantic). Won several Down Beat and Metronome awards; Esquire Silver Award, 1947.

TONY SCOTT (Anthony Sciacca), clarinet; b. Morristown, N. J., 1921. Clarinet at 12; fan of Hutchinrider, clarinetist in old Casa Loma band. Jammed at Village Vanguard while a student at Juilliard, 1940-42, studying harmony and theory. Army May '42-Nov. '45. W. Buddy Rich briefly, 1946, then w. Ben Webster, Ch. Ventura big band, Lecuona Cuban Band; with Sid Catlett at Spotlite on tenor sax; w. Babs Gonzales at Onyx, Carnegie concerts and theatre tour w. Billie Holiday, 1948; tour w. Frankie Laine. Joined C. Thornhill, Feb. 1949. Rec. w. Benny Carter, Kirby Walker (De Luxe); *Everything is Cool* w. Babs (Apollo); Bill de Arango session (Haven); own date on Gotham w. Dizzy, Trummy Young, Ben Webster, Sarah Vaughan, playing alto on *You're Only Happy When I'm Blue*, clarinet on *Ten Lessons with Timothy*. Fave: Benny Goodman, but his own style is bop.

GEORGE SHEARING, piano and accordion; b. Battersea, London, Eng., 1920. Linden Lodge School for the Blind; toured England with all-blind band, also worked w. Ambrose, Ted Heath and other leading British groups. Rec. for British Decca since 1938. Came to NYC 1946 for few months' visit; returned to England, but back in NYC Dec. 1947 to stay in USA permanently. Most of 1948 at Three Deuces with Oscar Pettiford & J. C. Heard; opened at Clique Club Dec. '48. Plays a very intense combination of chord and single-note bop piano styles, and is the first jazzman to feature genuine bop accordion. Has an album of piano solos on London label, recorded several years ago not in bop style. American recordings: *Have You Met Miss Jones,* etc. (Savoy). By far the greatest modern musician to come out of British jazz, he has written arrangements for Gene Williams and other bands. Discovery and MGM records, 1949.

JOHN SIMMONS, bass; b. Oklahoma, 1918. School in LA to 1936; discovered in San Diego by John Hammond, made first records w. Teddy Wilson in quartet date w. Harry James, Norvo, Aug. 1937 (Brunswick). W. King Cole, '37; Jimmy Bell, '38; Frank Derrick, '39; John Letman, '40; Roy Eldridge, '41; Benny Goodman, July '41; Louis Armstrong, '42; Eddie Heywood, '44; Ill. Jacquet, '46; various 52nd St. groups w. C. Hawkins, Sid Catlett, Don Byas. Also rec. w. Billie Holiday (Decca, Commodore). An early frequenter of Minton's from 1941 on.

SONNY STITT, alto sax. Exact information is scarce on this young artist owing to his incarceration on and off in the past two years. First heard of in Detroit, he appeared in Newark and NYC 1945-6 and impressed musicians as the first young alto star to simulate Bird's style effectively. Recorded for Savoy, with the Be Bop Boys, *Webb City* and *Fat Boy;* own session, *Blues in Bebop, Seven Up.* Also dates w. Kenny Clarke (Victor bop album), Lord Nelson, Russell, Jacquet (King), Dizzy Gillespie Musicraft small band date (*One Bass Hit, Oop Bop sh' Bam, That's Earl Brother, Hand Fulla Gimme*).

EARL SWOPE, trombone; b. Washington, D.C., 1922. Worked locally with Don Lamond's small group, also toured w. Sonny Dunham, Boyd Raeburn; Buddy Rich, 1947; Woody Herman, 1948-9. Rec. *Gabardine & Serge* w. Chaloff (Savoy); *Dateless Brown* w. Rich (Mercury); *Keen & Peachy, I've Got News for You* w. Woody (Col.).

"SIR" CHARLES THOMPSON, piano & arranger. First records while w. Lionel Hampton 1940-41, *Altitude, Chasin' with Chase,* etc. (Victor). W. Coleman Hawkins, 1944-5, made Asch album and Capitol dates; own all-star session for Apollo Sep. 1945 with Ch. Parker, Dexter Gordon *Takin' Off, If I Had You, 20th Century Blues, Street Beat.* Lucky Millinder, 1946. Illinois Jacquet, 1947; composed *Robbins Nest* and recorded it with Jacquet on Apollo. Mainly a Basie-style rather than a bop pianist.

ELI "LUCKY" THOMPSON, tenor; b. Detroit, June 1924. Studied Cass Tech. High; Francis Hellstein of Detroit Symphony, and also with father of trombonist Bobby Byrne; harmony and orch. under John Phelps. Left Detroit w. Trenier Twins' Bama State Collegians. Lionel Hampton 1943; settled in NYC, worked w. Ray Parker; w. Sid Catlett at Deuces; a month w. Don Redman, and later w. original Eckstine band incl. Diz, Bird, Millinder, Slam Stewart, Erroll Garner; a year with Basie, then settled on west coast, became most prolific jazz recording artist in LA; sessions and gigs w. Dizzy (Dial), Benny Carter, Louis Armstrong, Boyd Raeburn, Johnny Richards, Jimmy Mundy, Buddy Baker, Ike Carpenter, etc. Heard on practically all Exclusive Records 1945-6 in Buddy Baker backgrounds, groups, etc. Also acc. Dinah Washington (Apollo), Estelle Edson, Ivie Anderson (Black & White). Solos: *Taps Miller, Avenue C, I Didn't Know*

About You w. Basie; dates w. Lips Page (Continental), Dodo Marmarosa (Atomic). Own sessions on Excelsior and Victor (bebop album), best solo *Just One More Chance* (Victor). Also heard in Junior Jazz album (Black & White), Lyle Griffin (IRRA), Cliff Lange (Pan-American), Slim Gaillard (Majestic), Karl George *Cherokee* (Melodisc), Freddy Green (Duke), Willie Smith (Sunset). Earliest records are Lucky Millinder's *I Can't See For Looking* (Decca, May 1944), Lips Page (Commodore, March 1944). Smooth, pure tone and individual style distinguished him from both Hawkins and Lester Young schools. Esquire New Star award, 1947.

LENNIE TRISTANO, piano; b. Chicago, 1919. American Conservatory of Music in Chi. Local clubs and teaching until summer of 1946, when he came to New York at the instigation of Chubby Jackson; played with small groups in Freeport, N. Y. and 52nd Street, mostly with Billy Bauer, guitar, and Arnold Fishkin, bass. Many prominent musicians have studied harmony, theory and piano with Lennie, whose ideas extend far beyond bebop. An extraordinary musician whose work is worthy of deep study. Album for Keynote and session for Majestic, both sets of masters now owned by Mercury; also six sides for Disc and one side for Victor Modern Jazz Piano album. Favorite bop pianist: Bud Powell.

CHARLIE VENTURA (real name Venturo), tenor sax; b. Philly, Dec. 2, 1916; fourth from the top in a family of thirteen children. Got first sax, a C Melody, at 14. Listened to Chu Berry, jammed at local music shop with Bill Harris, worked in Dad's hat factory, and from 1940 to '42 at Philly Navy Yard, sitting in nights at the local Down Beat with Dizzy, Roy, De Franco, Vido Musso and other big jazz names. In '42, through Roy Eldridge and Teddy Walters, landed a job with Gene Krupa. Stayed (except for interlude with Teddy Powell while Gene was disbanded) until 1946, then had his own big band. (See Chapter 5). Shared a small unit with Chubby Jackson for a while, then started on his own, developed the bop style with horns and voices working in both unison and harmony; first with Buddy Stewart, then in 1948 with Jackie Cain and Roy Kral. Plays soprano, alto, tenor and baritone saxes. During 1948 his eight-piece group became the most popular small band in the country playing modern jazz.

Charlie's solos on records until 1947 didn't feature the bop style towards which he gradually evolved later. His biggest early hits were such flashy specialties as *Dark Eyes* and *Yesterdays*, recorded with Krupa. Dates with Neal Hefti (Keynote), Jazz at Phil. Vols. I & III (Asch), Timme Rosenkrantz (Continental), WNEW Vol. 2 (Vox), Teddy Wilson's *September Song, Time After Time* etc. (Musicraft). Under his own name, pick-up band dates for Sunset, Black and White (eight 12-inch and four 10-inch sides), an album for Lamplighter, a few sides on Savoy; 1946-48, own regular bands, big and small, on National and Sitting In, best sides include *11:60, East of Suez, Euphoria, I'm Forever Blowing Bubbles,* and his baritone sax solo *If I Had You.* Signed with Victor late in 1948.

GEORGE WALLINGTON (Figlia), piano; b. Palermo, Italy, 1923; father, an opera singer, brought family here a year later. Piano w. private teacher; gigs in Greenwich Village, where he met Max Roach, Bird, Benny Harris and Dizzy. Joined Diz's first band w. Oscar Pettiford at Onyx, 1944; w. Joe Marsala at Hickory House, various groups at Three Deuces incl. Ch. Parker, Geo. Auld, Red Rodney, Allen Eager. W. Kai Winding, 1948. Rec. *A Bar A Second, Gabardine & Serge* w. Chaloff (Savoy), *Jane's Bounce* etc. w. Eager (Savoy). Faves: Bud Powell, Al Haig. Comp. *Lemon Drop* rec. by Chubby Jackson (Rainbow).

CHUCK WAYNE (CHARLES JAGELKA), guitar; b. NYC, Feb. 27, 1923, son of a cabinet maker; Czech family. Picked up brother's mandolin while at junior high and started playing with a Russian balalaika band. When mandolin began to warp, threw it in the furnace and got a guitar. At 18, while running elevator for a living, met the late, great pianist Clarence Profit, and soon after was doubling between jobs with Profit's Trio at the Two O'Clock Club and the late Nat Jaffe's similarly-styled trio at Kelly's Stable. Later with Profit at the Red Rooster uptown. Army, Feb. '42-March '44, then w. Joe Marsala on and off for two years mostly at Hickory House. Also w. Phil Moore at Cafe Society; joined Woody Herman May '46, stayed until band broke up seven months later. Free-lancing since then with own groups, also Alvy West's Little Band, 1948, and Barbara Carroll Trio. Rec. w. Helen Humes (Savoy), Barney Bigard (Black & White), Sarah Vaughan, Slam Stewart (Continental). Solos: *Cherokee* w. Joe Marsala & Diz (Black & White), *Sidewalks of Cuba* w. Woody (Columbia); *East of the Sun* w. Lester Young (Aladdin), own comps. *Zero Hour* (Black & White) and *Slightly Dizzy* (Musicraft) both w. Marsala. Faves: Segovia, Ch. Christian. One of the two or three top bop guitar men, deserving of much more recognition than he has earned.

BEN WEBSTER, tenor sax; b. Kansas City, c. 1909. In New Mexico w. Gene Coy, 1929, then w. Jap Allen, Blanche Calloway, Andy Kirk; to NYC w. Benny Moten 1932; then w. Fletcher Henderson, Benny Carter, Willie Bryant Orch., 1934-5, later w. Cab Calloway. Duke Ellington, 1939-43, then own groups until rejoined Duke Nov. '48. Though not a bopper, has influenced and associated with many members of the new movement. Best rec. w. Duke (Victor) and own sessions on Savoy, Haven, Wax.

FREDDY WEBSTER, trumpet. Had own group around Ohio 1938-39; this included Tadd Dameron, on whom Webster was a main influence. W. Lucky

Millinder, Earl Hines, 1941; Lunceford, '42; Benny Carter, '43; back w. Lucky, '44, then various groups around New York; sat in w. Geo. Auld on Musicraft, but no solos; featured w. Frankie Socolow on *The Man I Love, Reverse the Charges* (Duke), Sarah Vaughan-Tadd Dameron *You're Not the Kind, If You Could See Me Now* (Musicraft). Died Chicago, 1947. According to Tadd, could have been one of the greatest men in jazz.

HAROLD "DOC" WEST, drums; b. Wolford, N. D., 1915. To Chicago 1926, studied piano, 'cello. Tiny Parham, 1932, Erskine Tate and other Chicago bands; Roy Eldridge, '37-8; in NYC, subbed for Chick Webb for several months before Webb's death. Back to Roy; briefly with Ellington, Basie. At Minton's with Monk, Nick Fenton, Kermit Scott, 1940. Several years on and off 52nd Street with Slam, Byas, Garner, Lester Young, Tiny Grimes, Roy et al. Many records with above groups on Savoy, Super-Disc, etc.; also *Body & Soul* date w. Billie Holiday (Vocalion) and *Bird's Nest* date w. Ch. Parker (Dial).

MARY LOU WILLIAMS, arranger, piano; b. Pittsburgh, 1910. Not a bop pianist, but a great modern stylist who has influenced many young musicians in favor of bop and started writing bop herself in 1947. Wrote bop arr. of *Stealing Apples* for Benny Goodman (Capitol). Rec. w. own groups on Victor, Asch, Disc, Continental.

KAI WINDING, slide and valve trombone; b. Aarhus, Denmark, May 18, 1922. To U. S. at 12; father w. Gen. Motors. Trombone at high school, NYC. Joined union to work with neighbor, Shorty Allen, opening Fiesta Danceteria, Times Square, in 1940 opposite Coleman Hawkins' big band. W. Bobby Day at Arcadia, Sonny Dunham, Alvino Rey. 1942, in Coast Guard, Curtis Bay, Md.; training station dance band under Bill Schallen to Oct. 1945. While in service rec. first solos on Manor 12-inch date w. Manor All Stars (Roy Stevens, trumpet, Ray Turner, tenor, Fred Otis, piano, Ch. Perry, drums). W. Benny Goodman to Jan. 1946—no solos on records. Stan Kenton until band broke up April '47; featured on *Artistry in Percussion, Bolero* and *Boogie, Collaboration* etc. W. Ch. Ventura to Feb. 1948, then w. Gene Ammons. Back in NYC, at Royal Roost w. Ch. Parker, Tadd Dameron. Records: *11:60, East of Suez* w. Ventura (National); Neal Hefti session (Keynote); own date on Savoy: *Always, Grab Your Ax Max, Loaded, Sweet Miss.* Teddy Reig date on Savoy: *Mr. Dues*, and valve trombone solo on *O-Go-Mo.* Solos on Five Bops' *Hot Halavah* (Sitting In), Coleman Hawkins *Bean A Re Bop* (Aladdin).

LESTER WILLIS "PRES" YOUNG, tenor sax; b. New Orleans, 1909. Father, originally a blacksmith, had studied at Tuskegee; played violin, was teacher, worked with choirs; taught Lester drums, later bought him alto sax.

Played baritone a while with the Bostonians; worked a year with King Oliver, then w. Walter Paige & His 13 Original Blue Devils, then to Kansas City, joined Benny Moten-George Lee group and first small Count Basie unit. Replaced Coleman Hawkins in Fletcher Henderson band 1934 and flopped because he didn't sound like Hawk. Few months w. Andy Kirk, then to Basie again at Reno Club, KC, summer 1936, then to Grand Terrace in Chicago. First record date with Jones-Smith Inc. (Count Basie Quintet) for Vocalion-Columbia, Oct. 9, 1936: *Shoe Shine Boy, Evenin', Lady Be Good, Boogie Woogie*. Left Basie Dec. 13, 1940; own band at Kelly's Stable w. Shad Collins, Clyde Hart, Johnny Collins, Nick Fenton, Harold West. Sat in often at Minton's, Nick's, Village Vanguard. March 1942, own small band jointly with brother, drummer Lee Young, in Los Angeles; to Cafe Society, NYC, Sept. '42. Back with Basie Dec. 1943 in LA, then 15 months in Army 1944-5. Several concert tours w. Norman Granz, then own small group. Says "Bop can be pretty, but I play a *swing* tenor." Lester was the key figure in the development of an easy-going, lag-along style and rather soft, flat tenor tone, as opposed to a hitting-it-on-the-nose style; in short, he was, with Charlie Christian and a few others, responsible for the change from hot jazz to cool jazz which is a vital feature of bebop, and though his style is not entirely bop, almost every young tenor player in recent years has modeled his style on "Pres" to some extent. Own fave records: *Taxi War Dance* w. Basie (Vocalion); *Back In Your Own Backyard* and *Sailboat In the Moonlight* w. Billie Holiday (Vocalion). Comp. *Tickle Toe,* rec. w. Basie (Col.). Clarinet solos w. Kansas City Six, Sept. 1938 (Commodore). Own album on Keynote; featured in tenor sax albums on Savoy; numerous small band dates on Philo-Aladdin. Lesser known early solos include *Blitzkrieg Baby* w. Una Mae Carlisle (Bluebird), *Things 'Bout Comin' My Way* w. Sam Price (Decca), *Upright Organ Blues* w. Glenn Hardman (Columbia). Innumerable small band dates in the late 1930's with Teddy Wilson, B. Holiday (Brunswick, Vocalion, Okeh) and in 1943-4 with Dickie Wells (Signature 12-inch), Johnny Guarnieri (Savoy). One date w. Benny Goodman, March 1938 (Victor). Several volumes of Jazz at Philharmonic. Appeared in *Jammin' The Blues* short made by Norman Granz and Gjon Mili.

DISCOGRAPHY

Following is a list of albums suitable for a general introduction to bebop. Most of them are still available at from $3 to $4 each.

CHARLIE CHRISTIAN MEMORIAL (VOX ESP 302)

NEW FIFTY SECOND STREET JAZZ (VICTOR HJ 9)

BEBOP (VICTOR P 226)

BEBOP (KEYNOTE K 140)

BEBOP (SAVOY S 506)

BEBOP JAZZ 1947 (DIAL D-1)

BEBOP JAZZ 1948 (DIAL D-2)

NEW SOUNDS IN MODERN MUSIC (SAVOY S-508)

THE PARKERS (SAVOY S-509)

DIZZY GILLESPIE AND HIS ALL STARS (MUSICRAFT S 7)

CHARLIE PARKER (SAVOY S-510)

———

Leonard Feather's "Jazz At Its Best" program is heard regularly on WMGM, New York.